MEN AND AFFAIRS

BOOKS BY WILLIAM BARCLAY
Published by The Westminster Press

Men and Affairs
The Men, The Meaning, The Message of the New Testament Books
New Testament Words
Introduction to the First Three Gospels
Introduction to John and the Acts of the Apostles
Marching On: Daily Readings for Younger People
Marching Orders: Daily Readings for Younger People
The Old Law & The New Law
And Jesus Said: A Handbook on the Parables of Jesus
God's Young Church
The King and the Kingdom
The First Three Gospels
Fishers of Men
Turning to God: A Study of Conversion in the Book of Acts and Today
Many Witnesses, One Lord
The All-Sufficient Christ: Studies in Paul's Letter to the Colossians
The Promise of the Spirit
Train Up a Child: Educational Ideals in the Ancient World
Daily Study Bible

MEN AND AFFAIRS

by

William Barclay

Edited by C. L. Rawlins

THE WESTMINSTER PRESS

Philadelphia

© A. R. Mowbray & Co. Ltd. 1977

Published by The Westminster Press ®
Philadelphia, Pennsylvania

PRINTED IN THE UNITED STATES OF AMERICA

9   8   7   6   5   4   3   2   1

Library of Congress Cataloging in Publication Data

Barclay, William, lecturer in the University of Glasgow.
  Men and affairs.

  Bibliography: p.
  1. Christian biography — Book reviews.
  2. Christianity — 20th century — Book reviews. 3. Books
  — Reviews. I. Title.
  BR1700.2.B35   209′.2′2 [B]   78-1926
  ISBN 0-664-24203-0

CONTENTS

2. The Affairs of Man

3. The things of God

EDITOR'S PREFACE

Professor William Barclay has been hailed as the world's best-selling religious author. He is just that. Few religious writers, still less professors of Biblical learning, have been so affected by *cacoethes scribendi*—the penman's itch—as he. If 'purity of heart is to will one thing' then surely he is of heart most pure, for his life may be seen as a single-minded devotion to understand and communicate the truth and present-day reality of Jesus Christ. The resultant list of more than fifty books, not to mention the countless articles, demonstrates his achievement.

This year Dr. Barclay celebrates his seventieth birthday. We rejoice with him, and with his wife, family and very many friends around the world. Retired now from active academic life, though happily for us not from literary activity, it is a time to look back and reflect. William Barclay has himself done this in his moving autobiographical reminiscences†, and others, too, have added their own considerations‡. It is right that this should be done: we are meant to take God's gifts and servants seriously, and in William Barclay we have a servant of His word and of His people *par excellence*. But it should not be overlooked that as well as being a great author Barclay is himself an experienced reviewer, bookman and religious littérateur. Long before he wrote his first book he was writing of other authors, and he has done so ever since—regularly, perceptively, candidly, yet always kindly. The *traits* which make him such a fine and able writer also characterize him as a reviewer. Let us note four of them:

There is, firstly, his *simplicity*. Oscar Wilde made a point when he observed that the truth is rarely pure and never simple; Dr. Barclay demonstrates repeatedly that this was no more than a half truth, and carefully fulfils Einstein's exhortation that everything should be made as simple as possible, but not simpler. He is never simplistic. Secondly, there is his *directness*. He immediately gets to the heart of the matter, there is no verbiage, he does not indulge in paraphrastics or sunny clichés. His matter is described in bold strokes: the outline, the detail and—it is never wanting—the application. He supplies no opiates but

---

† *Testament of Faith* was published by A. R. Mowbray & Co. Ltd., 1975.
‡ *See* David Edwards in the Preface to *Testament of Faith;* Johnston R. McKay's 'Personal Appreciation' in *Biblical Studies in Honour of William Barclay*, 1976; and the late Ronald Falconer on 'Barclay the Broadcaster' in that same volume.

calls and recalls to the stern demands of real discipleship. Then, thirdly, there is his superb facility for *illustration*. Because he is gifted with a remarkable memory, his writings sparkle with apposite quotations and pointed anecdotes. Some complain of his 'liberalism', others of his conservatism! none of his dullness, for dull he cannot be. His writings *are* enjoyable! Even in his most serious moods—and he can be very serious—there is a hopeful joy which underpins his work; a joy which is contagious. But lastly, and above all, he writes as one *in love with Jesus Christ*. His work is energized by an ongoing experience of his Lord. Some write of the Bible as an historical document, others as a theological treatise, yet others as if it were a legal code; Barclay writes otherwise: conscious and supportive of its historicity, careful of and humbly seeking its deeper truth, mindful of its ethical imperatives—and ever zealous to preserve their sharpness—his writings reflect a grateful and adoring response to the love of God in Christ Jesus. It is this which ultimately inspires his thought, and this which has kept him at it for over forty years, expounding, commenting and reviewing.

The reviews which are gathered here were previously published in *The Expository Times*. Many of them are biographical, some are frankly secular; all of them reflect Dr. Barclay's wide interests and rich humanity. Some of the books are now out of print but they are nevertheless characteristic of the period in which they were written and the movement of thought therein. Other editors may well have selected or reduced them differently. I hope, however, that they will be found worthy of their author and of interest to those who, like me, have found them month by month over many years to be an important and necessary part of one's spiritual diet.

Acknowledgments are gratefully made to Messrs. T. & T. Clark Ltd., the proprietors of *The Expository Times*, and to Dr. Leslie Mitton its former editor; to Richard Mulkern, Managing Director of A. R. Mowbray and Co. Ltd., a wise and patient friend; to Mrs. Carol Rogers and her colleagues at the Reference Library, Birmingham; to my wife Veronica who cheerfully shoulders extra work that I may enjoy and explore the fruits of the spirit; but above all, to Professor Barclay himself who makes available with such prodigious and kindly effort the ripe fruits of his learning.

Clive Rawlins

I The Men of Affairs

MR. BUCHAN, WRITER
Arthur C. Turner

Mr. Turner writes with an easy mastery of his material, with a charm and lightness of style, and with such an obvious and infectious enthusiasm for his subject that this is a fascinating book.

What an amazing career John Buchan had! Born in a Scottish manse, he was President of the Oxford Union, publisher's reader for John Lane at the astonishingly early age of twenty, possessor of the dignity of a paragraph in 'Who's Who' at the age of twenty-three, barrister, one of Milner's young men in South Africa, publisher, Colonel in the Intelligence Corps, Director of Information in the 1914–18 War, Lord High Commissioner of the Church of Scotland, Companion of Honour, Doctor of Civil Laws of Oxford University, intimate friend of Ramsay Macdonald and President Roosevelt, Chancellor of Edinburgh University, and Governor-General of Canada. It is a staggering record of achievement to pack into any one life.

Even more amazing is the astonishing versatility of his mind. In the record of his literary works there are listed twenty-four novels; four volumes of short stories; two books of stories for children; twenty-three volumes of history, biography, and belles-lettres; two volumes of verse; and one of autobiography. And to these must be added countless contributions to periodical literature. There can be few men who have produced a volume on 'The Taxation of Foreign Income', an adventure novel like 'Greenmantle', and a biography like 'Sir Walter Scott'. There is something Elizabethan in this man who was scholar, soldier, statesman, churchman, proconsul, and author.

He began with the great advantage of having been born in a Scottish manse. As Mr. Turner says, 'It is indeed hardly surprising that so many famous men have been sons of the manse, for to be brought up in a Church family is to have, quite informally, an education at once cultured and practical, and to enjoy a respect that is wholly dependent on the performance of duties, which does not shut one off from any class in society but brings one into contact with all.' Further, until late in his life, he had an inspiration in his mother. 'He wrote a letter to his mother every day; he did so from his first leaving home until the end of her life. The note was written every day immediately after breakfast, and was the first duty of the day.' Still further, few men can have organized their lives like John Buchan. 'His daily routine afforded him six clear hours of work, and he put in that amount of work *every day*; such persistence is infinitely more effective than spasmodic effort, however great.

Mr. Turner has done us a real service and given us a great deal of pleasure by writing this book,[1] for he has told us of a life which reads like one of Buchan's own adventure novels and which is an inspiration to others.

Here William Barclay reviews with relish a biography of a fellow Scot who was clearly much to his taste— John Buchan, who was famous in his day, not only as a distinguished public figure, but also as a writer of thrillers—The Thirty-nine Steps is probably the best remembered of his twenty-four novels. But Barclay is also being perhaps unconsciously

[1] Published by SCM PRESS in their 'Torch Biographies' series, 1949.

autobiographical in this review. True, he was not himself a son of a Scottish manse; but he was, for many years, Minister at Trinity Church, Renfrew. He notes, too, how Buchan found inspiration in his mother. This has been a feature of Barclay's own life, as readers of his autobiography Testament of Faith, written many years after this review, will remember. And his praise of John Buchan for his ability to maintain a steady daily discipline of work reflects also a marked feature of Barclay's own life.

BOOKER T. WASHINGTON
Basil T. Mathews

Booker T. Washington was born a slave. He knew neither the date of his birth nor his father's name. There was a time when Booker T. Washington had, as it were, a price ticket on him, for in the records of Franklin County there is a list of ten slaves of James Burroughs with their assessed value. Booker was priced at 400 dollars, his elder brother, John, at 550 dollars, his little sister, Amanda, at 200 dollars, while Jane, their mother, was valued at 250 dollars.

The coming of freedom to the slaves brought many more problems than it solved; and to Washington was given the task of seeking and finding a solution to many of these problems. From his earliest days he had a passion for education. He heard of the Hampton Institute where negroes might be educated. He set out to go to it and in the end got there, penniless and in rags and tatters.

Having absorbed all that Hampton Institute could give him Washington taught here and there, but his great work was done at Tuskegee with which his name will always be connected. He had to start from absolutely nothing. He had even to learn to make the bricks from which his buildings were constructed. All kinds of people gave gifts. 'No gift touched Booker quite so deeply as that of an old, illiterate ex-slave woman, in rags, but cleanly, who hobbled into the schoolroom one day, leaning on a cane and said, "I ain't got no money, but I want you to take these six eggs . . . and I wants you to put these six eggs into de eddication o' dese boys an' gals".'

Tuskegee grew until it numbered its students by the thousands, and behind it all was Booker Washington. One of his right-hand men said of him, 'We often reason that we can't do a thing because we haven't done it. He himself did, and called on us to do what had been done. He paid no attention to what had not been done elsewhere'. It was always the future in which he was interested. He was a master of detail. All his colleagues got notes from him about the smallest matter. Even his wife was not exempt.

Booker Washington had a gift for memorable sayings, 'No man shall drag me down by making me hate him.' 'No race can prosper till it learns that there is as much dignity in tilling a field as in writing a poem.' 'There are two ways of exerting one's strength—one is pushing down, the other is pulling up.' 'The world looks more hopeful and more filled with God's providence when you are at the bottom looking up than when you are at the top looking down.'

In writing this book[1] Basil Mathews has had access to many original records, letters and documents, besides having had many conversations with those who knew Booker Washington. He has produced a book of absorbing interest, a book which the reader will find it hard to put down once he has taken it up.

It is a stern test of a review that it should not only read interestingly years after it was written, but also that it should still attract the reader strongly to the book which was its subject. This review of a 'life' of Booker T. Washington the ex-slave who, both by achievement and strength of character, has assuredly earned a place among the great men of the

[1] Published by SCM Press.

United States, triumphantly passes this test. This is all the more so in the light of the excitement surrounding Roots, *by Alex Harvey and its subsequent controversy. Clearly, Barclay enjoyed some of what he calls the 'memorable sayings' of Booker* Washington, one of which, notable and dateless, is this: '*The world looks more hopeful and more filled with God's providence when you are at the bottom looking up, than when you are at the top looking down*'.

PLAIN MR. KNOX
Elizabeth Whitley

To choose a great subject is to be half-way to writing a great book; and quite certainly it would take a genius in dullness to write a dull book about John Knox. Mrs. Whitley has produced a biography which is as thrilling and interesting as any novel.[1]

John Knox began as a priest of the Roman Catholic Church; the day came when in the Church of England he refused the offer of a bishopric; and he was in the end the creator of Presbyterianism in Scotland.

Knox was a man of power. When he was called, all against his will, to be a minister of St. Andrews and when he preached they said of him: 'Others shed the branches of Papistry, but he strikes at the root'. 'To argue with Knox', sighed Maitland, 'is like a foretaste of Judgment Day.' 'The voice of one man', said Randolph, 'is able in one hour to put more life in us than five hundred trumpets continually blustering in our ears.'

Knox was a man of courage. After one of his battles with Queen Mary, she blazed at him: 'Ye will not always be at your book.' So she turned her back on him. But Knox departed with 'a reasonable merry countenance'. Whereat some papists, offended, said: 'He is not afraid'.

Knox was a man of utter sincerity. Carlyle said of him: 'He clung to sincerity as a drowning man to a cliff'. 'Neither hatred nor favour to any causeth me this day to speak, but only the obedience which I owe unto God.'

He had a magnificent power of invective. He said of Gardner that he was 'son of Satan, brother to Cain, and fellow to Judas the traitor'. Sometimes that power ran away with him as it did in his *First Blast of the Trumpet* when he spoke of 'this monstriferous empire of Women'. 'To promote a Woman to bear rule ... above any realm, nation or city is repugnant to Nature; contumely to God ... and the subversion of all good order, equity and justice. ...' Mrs. Whitley shrewdly remarks that it is not irrelevant to remember that Knox was living with his mother-in-law when he wrote this and having 'troubles domestical, whereof being unaccustomed I am the more fearful'!

He was an astonishing democrat. Did he not give to kirk sessions the dangerous responsibility of taking heed 'to the life, manners, diligence and study of their ministers. If he be worthy of admonition, they must admonish him; of correction, they must correct him'?

He was, it must never be forgotten, a sick man in constant pain after the torture of the galleys. There are letters in which the writing trails away because of the ague which so often shook him. 'At midnight', says the indomitable workman, 'I write with sleepand eyes.'

Like all great men, he had a great sense of his own destiny. 'I was a watchman', he says, 'both over the Realm and over the Kirk of God gathered within the same.'

Mrs. Whitley has drawn a vivid picture of a great man, for she writes with verve and scholarship combined.

Here is another review which has worn astonishingly well partly, no doubt, because the subject of it is great

[1] Published by SKEFFINGTON & CO., 1960.

enough to be timeless. 'It would take a genius in dullness', Barclay says, 'to write a dull book about John Knox.' By the same token it could also be said that it would be almost impossible for William Barclay to write a dull review on a book about John Knox. The subject is obviously greatly to his taste as Knox was not only a Scot, but also a man of destiny and power, as well as a massive figure of the Reformation. Here again Barclay's eye and fondness for the apt quotation is apparent. Thus he repeats Carlyle's aphorism on Knox: 'he clung to sincerity as a drowning man to a cliff'.

WASHINGTON: THE INDISPENSABLE MAN
J. T. Flexner

When a man has written a four-volume biography of a person, if he sits down to distil the essence of his four volumes into one, he has undertaken a difficult task. That is the task which James Thomas Flexner has taken, and he has achieved it with conspicuous success.[1] In war and in peace Washington was indeed the indispensable man.

In the first place, Washington had a presence. He was six feet two, with the body of an athlete. When he was only twenty-one he 'carried the manifest air of one born to command'. 'Not a king in Europe', it was said of him, 'but would look like a *valet de chambre* by his side.' And there was his charm. On meeting him Abigail Adams quoted to her husband what the Queen of Sheba said of Solomon: 'The half was not told me'. He enjoyed flirtatious banter. 'He can be down right impudent sometimes', wrote the wife of a Virginian colonel to one of her friends, 'such impudence, Fanny, as you and I like.'

He had extraordinary physical courage. In battle he seemed to have a charmed life. Once he had to have an operation for a tumour on his thigh. It was in the days long before there were any anaesthetics. When the opening was made it was seen that the trouble was more deeply seated than had been expected. The younger surgeon quailed at the task before him. 'Cut away', the older surgeon said. 'Deep—deeper—deeper still. Don't be afraid. You see how well he bears it.'

He was very fond of entertaining and being entertained. In 1768 he went to Church on fifteen days and hunted foxes on forty-nine. He attended three balls, two plays and one horse race. He was temperamentally a gambler, in the early days at cards, and in the later days in battle. In the seven years between 1768 and 1775 he entertained about 2000 guests. None was ever turned away from his home in Mount Vernon, 'lest the deserving suffer'. His entertaining was simple. 'My manner of living is plain. I do not mean to be put out of it. A glass of wine and a bit of mutton are always ready, and such as are content to take of them are welcome.'

He was a great chairman and president, for he had in a superlative degree 'the gift of finding beneath controversy common ground'. 'It was his genius to reach, by recognizing the essence of a problem, the bedrock that underlay opposites.'

As he grew older his sight failed. Once he was making a speech. It was not having the effect he would have liked. At the end of it he thought that he would read a private letter to his audience. He came to a complete stop. He then produced from his pocket something that practically no one had ever seen him use before, a pair of spectacles. 'Gentlemen', he said, 'You will permit me to put on my spectacles, for I have not only grown grey but almost blind in the service of my country.' At that even his hardened soldiers wept—and the day was saved.

On his death bed he had only one fear, that he might be buried alive, and he gave strict instructions that his body must be kept for three days before it was buried.

It is a fitting tribute to a man who was one of the world's heroes.

On the whole, over the years, Barclay has been a kindly reviewer.

[1] Published by WM. COLLINS & SONS.

9

Not for him the tearing to shreds and the total or even partial destruction of some of his subjects. Thus, in this review of the leader of the American Revolution, he notes the difficulty which the author has had in condensing a four volume biography into one. Beyond that—and he claims that even this has been achieved with 'conspicuous success'—he is lenient. The contemporary reader, however, might well feel that there is more to be said about Washington than such domestic details as, for example, that 'in 1768 he went to Church on fifteen days and hunted foxes on forty-nine . . .'. Or that at Mount Vernon none was ever turned away from his home. It could also have been said that he kept slaves, and had a harsh side to his character.

ST. BERNARD OF CLAIRVAUX
E.T. by Geoffrey Webb and Adrian Walker

Any man who wrote hymns like 'Jesus, the very thought of Thee', 'Jesus, Thou Joy of loving hearts', 'Light of the anxious heart', 'O Jesus, King most wonderful' has, indeed, written his name across the devotions of the Church. It was Bernard of Clairvaux who wrote these hymns. It sometimes happens that the life of a great man goes back to some ancient document which is the basis of all biographies. It is so with Bernard, for his life goes back to the *Vita Prima Bernardi* composed by his contemporaries William of St. Thierry, Arnold of Bonnevaux, Geoffrey and Philip of Clairvaux, and Odo of Deuil. Strangely enough this ancient life has never until now appeared in English.[1]

The *Vita Prima* was the product of love; it is the experience of their friend Bernard that in it its writers have left to us. 'If only', said Geoffrey, 'I had been a greater spirit so that I might have received more of all that he tried to put into me!'

Bernard was born in a castle and he was the son of Tescelin, a soldier. His mother Aleth was a saint of God. She had six sons who all became monks and one daughter who became a nun.

It was at Cîteaux that Bernard in A.D. 1113 first entered on the monastic life. He was the means of taking all his brothers with him. Such was his magnetism that 'mothers hid their sons when Bernard came near, and wives clung to their husbands to prevent them from going to hear him'.

When he first went to Clairvaux, a new foundation, he was a man without sympathy. He was himself of such purity that all avoided him. When men confessed their faults to him they found as little sympathy as there is between light and darkness.

His words sowed the seeds of despair in the weaker brothers. But then he began to see that his monks were mere men, and daily he grew in loving sympathy, until Clairvaux became what William of St. Thierry called 'a school of love', where 'the study of love is pursued, love's disputations held, love's questions answered'.

But this ascetic drove his frail body as if he had been a pillar of strength. He became one of the world's mightiest preachers. But above all he became the great mediator who again and again was called in to settle the disputes of the Church. He was haunted by the sense of the unity of the Church. When Pierleone, the false Pope, rent the Church in two, Bernard did not want to intervene, but he did: 'I see the seamless robe that none, Jew or pagan, dare rend on Calvary, torn to pieces by Pierleone. We have one faith, one Lord, one baptism.'

In the end the frail body gave out and the weary spirit found rest. 'He had exchanged death for life, and the light of faith for the fulfilled vision. His pilgrimage was over, and he had gone from this world to the Father.'

The makers of this translation have rendered to the Church a very real service. The *Vita Prima* was a labour of love, and so also we think is this translation of it—and we are grateful for it, for to know a saint better is always something for which to thank God.

Here is an example of how much information about his subject Barclay

[1] Published by A. R. MOWBRAY & CO. LTD., 1960.

can condense into a short space. Bernard of Clairvaux is a towering figure in Christian history. But it is clear that one of his great attractions for Barclay is that he was not only a healer of divisions in the Church but also one who, in his contacts with other men, learned the hard way to live in love and charity. Barclay has never advocated an emasculated Christianity. The ruggedness of his Highland background ever sharpens his application and interests.

KAGAWA OF JAPAN
C. J. Davey

It is given to very few men to become a legend within their own lifetime, but that was a greatness achieved by the humblest of men, by Toyohiko Kagawa of Japan.

It was in loneliness that Kagawa grew up, and it was Kagawa's youthful tragedy that his father and his mother died within weeks of each other and he grew up alone.

He was a brilliant and diligent pupil at school and at college, and it was through his desire to learn English that he first made accidental contact with Christianity in the person of Dr. Harry Myers, a Presbyterian missionary. It was the Cross which won Kagawa. He already knew the story of Jesus 'who loved men, specially the unhappy ones'. Then one day he heard the story of the Cross. 'Is this true?' he asked. 'Quite true', said the missionary. 'Jesus died?' Kagawa said. Myers looked at the stricken boy. 'He died because He loved them', he said. That night Kagawa prayed his first and his constant prayer, 'Oh, God, make me like Christ!'

He was a brilliant student. 'Books were always sure company. He made up his mind to take one down (from the library shelves) and read it through every day before he went to sleep.' But, scholar though he was, and still greater scholar though he was to be, his passion was for involvement in the human situation. The Japanese Church tended to be pietistic; he was determined to involve it in 'the joyful and dirty business of living'. Evangelism for him had to be matched with compassion'. Love for him was the master passion. 'Penniless and without food I can live', he said. 'Penniless I can share my rags. But I cannot bear to hear hungry children cry.'

So he crossed the river in Kobe and went to live in the terrible Shinkawa slum. He went to live in a filthy hut six feet by nine, the stench of which made his stomach heave. All around were 'murderers, pick-pockets, gamblers, epileptics, prostitutes, drunkards, rag-pickers'. Into his hut there came a man suffering from head to foot with a loathsome dermatitis and Kagawa shared his bed with him. He lived love and preached love.

In due time he was to marry Haru Shiba, 'Miss Spring', and their honeymoon was spent in the Shinkawa slum, living on £3 a month, 'taking their turn at a waterhydrant and a toilet which each served a hundred people'.

Kagawa was to become a great scholar, a doctor of philosophy, the founder of Japanese Trades Unions, a famous author, the friend and helper of the great, but he remained always the same.

He was fantastically generous, although he himself wore the poorest clothes and ate the cheapest food.

Mr. Davey has done a magnificent job in this book.[1] May it sell by the thousand and be read by tens of thousands, for this is a book about a man in whom something of Christ lived again.

That great Christian Toyohiko Kagawa later Minister of Agriculture, and once a household name in the West, has become somewhat obscured in the general Christian mind, perhaps due to the traumatic events of the Second World War. But it is good to be reminded, as this review does, of how the Christian

[1] Published by EPWORTH PRESS, 1960.

greatness of Kagawa was founded upon an encounter with the cross of Christ. It is clear that this book strongly commended itself to Barclay because, among other things, it was 'about a man in whom something of Christ lived again, which is constantly Barclay's definition of a saint.

WILLIAM CAREY
J. B. Middlebrook

William Paton once said that 'the missionary movement had not yet caught up with William Carey'. Carey was born in 1761 and to mark the bicentenary of his birth Mr. Middlebrook has produced a short but fascinating study of him.[1]

Few men ever did such a day's work as Carey, and he did it with a kind of unstoppable perseverance. 'I can plod', he said, 'I can persevere in any definite pursuit. To this I owe everything.'

He was a humble man. 'If God used *me*', he said, 'no one need despair.' He began life as a cobbler, and Sidney Smith dismissed him as 'the consecrated cobbler'.

He was by no means a religious young man, and the world owes William Carey to a fellow-apprentice called John Warr who pestered him into accompanying him to a meeting-house. When Carey began his ministry he was haunted by the thought of the regions beyond.

At last he moved a group of like-minded young men to action, chief of whom was Andrew Fuller. India was chosen; £130 was the total capital available. 'We saw', said Andrew Fuller, 'that there was a gold mine in India, and that it was as deep as the centre of the earth.' We asked, 'Who will venture to explore it?' 'I will venture to go down,' replied Carey, 'but remember you must hold the ropes.' So Carey went and at home his friends 'held the ropes'.

Of all amazing things about Carey the most amazing was his gift for languages. He tells us of a day in his life. He rose before 6 a.m.; read a chapter in Hebrew; conducted prayers in Bengali; read a portion of the Scripture in Hindustani; after breakfast did some translating from Sanskrit, and read a little Persian with munshi, after dinner translated part of Matthew into Sanskrit; at 6 p.m. sat down with a pundit to learn Telinga; and in the evening went on with translating Ezekiel into Bengali. It was said of him that 'he wore out three pundits in a day'. He translated the whole Bible into Bengali, Oriya, Hindi, Marathi, and Sanskrit. He set up his famous printing press and cut the first wooden type with his own hands.

He never preached hell-fire and hardly ever mentioned it. 'I have a strong persuasion', he said, 'that the doctrine of a dying Saviour would under the Holy Spirit's influence melt their hearts.'

Carey had his troubles. His first marriage was unhappy because his wife was mentally unbalanced. The Church at home in the end parted company with him and at least to some extent misunderstood him, for preaching the gospel meant so many things to him. He never once came home on furlough.

He died full of years and honour. To him Christ was everything. He said of his own distinguished son Felix that 'he shrivelled to an ambassador'!

He who reads this book—and may many read it—will think not of the greatness of Carey, but of the greatness of Jesus Christ.

Some words of Carey's, the onetime Northampton cobbler who became one of the world's greatest missionary figures, may well be quoted of Barclay himself; 'I can plod. I can persevere in any definite pursuit. To this I owe everything'. It is this combination of native genius with immense perseverance which has enabled a steady output

[1] Published by CAREY-KINGSGATE PRESS, 1961.

from Barclay over the years. Not that he would wish to be compared with so towering a figure as Carey. But it is clear that the great missionary means much to him, as he reviews this bi-centenary study, for a reason summed up in the concluding sentence of this review: 'he who reads this book —and may many read it—will think not of the greatness of Carey, but of the greatness of Jesus Christ'. As with Teilhard de Chardin (see p. 35 below), the centrality of Christ lies firmly at the heart of Barclay's work.

DOCTOR SANGSTER
Paul Sangster

'Sons in general make poor biographers.' That is a quotation from Paul Sangster's biography of his father.[1] However true that may be as a general statement, it is certainly not true in this particular case. Paul Sangster was the man to write this biography, firstly, because his father asked him to do it when he was near the end, and asked him to do it 'warts and all'. Secondly, it is clear that seldom have father and son been closer together. In a serious illness when his life was in peril, and when he was barely conscious, Paul Sangster remembers being aware of his father at the foot of his bed, and of hearing him say: 'I can't help you. Why can't I help you? Son, I'd go to hell for you if it would help.' This is one of the great *personal* biographies with nothing of the portentiousness of 'official' biographies but with all the intimacy of love.

Dr. Sangster came from a comparatively poor and humble home, and from the highly evangelical atmosphere of Radnor Street Mission. For long he was himself poor. His first guinea for supply was spent on a shirt, and his first article was written to buy his wife a new dress.

Dr. Sangster was a curious and a unique mixture. He was in many ways an ultra-evangelical. He agreed wholeheartedly with Wesley's description of the preacher's work: 'You have nothing to do but to save souls'. And yet no man had ever a stronger sense of the social gospel. When the basement of Westminster Chapel became an air raid shelter in the War time, his motto was, 'Service before services', and he never forced religion on people until they asked.

Again, he was one of the world's great preachers, but to this he added an extraordinary pastoral sense. The people he helped were legion. Jessie in hospital, a young girl, was going blind. 'Mr. Sangster', she said, 'God is going to take my sight away'. He did not answer for a little while. Then, 'Don't let Him, Jessie. Give it to Him.'

He died of progressive muscular atrophy all too soon, humanly speaking. As he grew more and more helpless, he wrote: 'I have made some resolutions—I will never complain. I will keep the home bright. I will count my blessings. I will try to turn it to gain.' He lived like a warrior and died like a saint.

A strange thing happened to me as I read this book. I began to have the feeling that Sangster might have done more had he not been such a tornado of energy, rushing from town to town and from continent to continent to preach. I wondered how to say so. And lo and behold, near the end of the book I discovered that Sangster had made the same discovery himself. 'I rushed about too much. I talked too much. I was proud of my health and work. I never had time really to look. The trouble was in the will—I lashed the body on, imprisoned in a time-table.'

Here W. E. Sangster lives again— and I think that he would have been abundantly satisfied with the way in which his son has fulfilled the trust committed to him.

There is a very discerning passage in this review of Paul Sangster's biography of his father, the great Methodist preacher of a few years ago, and probably one of the last of the princes of the pulpit. 'A strange thing happened to me as I read this book', Barclay

[1] Published by EPWORTH PRESS, 1969.

17

says. It was the feeling that Sangster might have done more had he rushed about less. 'I lashed the body on, imprisoned to a timetable', Sangster says. It is indeed perceptive of Barclay to have so clearly focused on so important an aspect of the life of one who was a great Christian, and a great man. Sangster had learned the truth about himself not so much through his oratory as through the suffering which came towards the end of his life. Barclay, too, has suffered.

COURAGE TO CHANGE
June Bingham

It might well be said that there is no better way of finding out what kind of man a man is than by listening to his prayers. In 1934 Reinhold Niebuhr used a pulpit prayer of which a friend asked for and kept a copy: 'O God, give us serenity to accept what cannot be changed, courage to change what should be changed, and wisdom to distinguish the one from the other'. There can be few better expressions of Reinhold Niebuhr's philosophy of life—and when he prayed that prayer for the first time he little knew how much need he would need to pray it. Mrs. Bingham has given us a full-length study of the life and thought of Reinhold Niebuhr, and if ever a book was written *con amore* this one is.[1]

The extraordinary thing about Reinhold Niebuhr is the width of his appeal. A thoughtful, but non-practising, Jew said: 'Reinie is my rabbi'. Walter Lippmann places Niebuhr 'in the very highest ranks of thinkers in this country during this century'. A hard-bitten politician says: 'Somehow when Reinie is preaching, I want to cry; but when he is through, I want to get out there and fight'.

It may be that his fascination is due to the fact that faith has never been easy for him. In an attack upon him Professor Carnell said: 'An undercurrent of scepticism runs through the entire theology of Niebuhr'. That was meant to be an accusation; it may well be the secret of Niebuhr's power. After Niebuhr had preached one Sunday Supreme Court Justice Felix Frankfurter stopped. 'I like what you said, Reinie', he said, 'and I speak as a believing unbeliever'. 'I'm glad you did', Niebuhr answered, 'for I spoke as an unbelieving believer.'

There is in Niebuhr an uncompromising honesty with himself and with other people. All unexpectedly Sloane Coffin invited him to Union. Niebuhr asked him what on earth he considered him able and equipped to teach. Coffin answered simply: 'You can't teach anything but just what you think', and Niebuhr never did.

His honesty made him hate self-righteousness. From what Niebuhr says it could be argued 'that the person who breaks one of the Ten Commandments may well end up less sinful than the person who self-righteously denounces people who break a Commandment'. 'If', says Niebuhr, 'there were a drunken orgy somewhere, I would bet ten to one a church member was not in it. But if there were a lynching, I would bet ten to one a church member was in it'. 'Not much evil is done by evil men', he said. 'Most evil is done by good people who do not know that they are not good.'

Space fails to tell of Niebuhr's illness which should have left him with his faculties impaired and which left him even greater to think and to help than he had ever been. To the analysis of life the man has added the conquest of life.

Here is a book, as easy to read as any novel, which gives a full-length picture of a great thinker, a great teacher, a great fighter and a good man. June Bingham has been lucky in her subject; Reinhold Niebuhr has been lucky in his biographer.

From this review of an important biography of the theologian, Reinhold Niebuhr, it is clear that a quality of Niebuhr's mind holds great attraction for Barclay. It is equally clear that the

[1] Published by SCM PRESS, 1961.

mental struggles to believe, which were a feature of Nicbuhr, likewise have great appeal for Barclay. Here again his felicity in selecting the apt quotation is marked: 'most evil is done by good people who do not know that they are not good'. Conquest through suffering, as with the previous piece, is seen as the fruitful means whereby reality is perceived, and truth appropriated.

MOODY WITHOUT SANKEY: A NEW AND BIOGRAPHICAL PORTRAIT

J. C. Pollock

'He put one hand on Britain and the other on America and lifted them both nearer to God.' There can seldom have been a higher tribute paid to a man than that, and that tribute was paid to D. L. Moody—and it was true.

Moody began as a go-getting shoe-salesman who wanted to be a millionaire. And it was in a shoe-shop that a word from Edward Kimball converted him. When that conversion happened Moody said: 'I thought the old sun shone a good deal brighter than it ever had before —I thought it was just smiling upon me; and as I walked out upon Boston Common, and heard the birds singing in the trees, I thought they were all singing a song to me. Do you know I fell in love with the birds. I had never cared for them before. It seemed to me I was in love with all creation. I had not a bitter feeling against any man, and I was ready to take all men to my heart'. And that remained true of Moody all his life.

Make no mistake, Moody did convert men and women. The 'New York Times', at first hostile and contemptuous, was in the end moved to say: 'The drunken have become sober, the vicious virtuous, the worldly and self-seeking unselfish, the ignoble noble, the impure pure, the youth have started with more generous aims, the old have been stirred from grossness. A new hope has lifted up hundreds of human beings, a new consolation has come to the sorrowful, and a better principle has entered the sordid life of the day'.

Yet Moody was by no means the typical evangelist. 'He could not have been pompous if he tried.' One of the journalists who covered one of his tours afterwards said: 'D. L. Moody with all his real piety is sometimes *unbearably* funny'.

Platitudinous piety had no part in Moody's life. His mind worked like lightning, and he had the gift of repartee. Once a heckler nearly wrecked a meeting and afterwards came up to shake hands. 'Are you going to preach to the miserable poor?' an aunt asked him as he left for Britain. 'Yes, and to the miserable rich, too', came the flashing reply. He abominated long and unctuous prayers. 'I tell you, friends', he said, some people's prayers need to be cut at both ends and set fire to in the middle.' Gladstone envied Moody his magnificent voice. 'I wish I had your chest, Mr. Moody', he said. Back came the answer: 'And I wish I had your head on top of it!'

He was the humblest of men. Once he picked up a handful of earth and ran it through his fingers and said: 'There's nothing more than *that* to D. L. Moody except as God uses him!' Above all he was the apostle of the love of God.

To read this book is to see Moody not only as a great evangelist but also as a great human being; we are grateful to Mr. Pollock for this vivid, dramatic and well-documented life of one who was undoubtedly a very great Christian and a very great man.

Mass evangelism has been a notable export of the United States to Britain for well over a century. Thus Moody and Sankey in Victorian times made an impact as great, if not even greater, than Billy Graham in ours. So this review of a book about Moody is of considerable and lasting

[1] Published by HODDER & STOUGHTON, 1966.

21

interest. And here again Barclay cannot resist the pleasure of repeating a telling quotation, as when Moody said 'some people's prayers need to be cut at both ends and set fire to in the middle'! This is so typical of

Barclay's prayers, which have been of such immense help to so many throughout the world. Directness, economy of expression, simplicity and dependence upon God are their principle features.

F. M. DOSTOEVSKY: HIS IMAGE OF MAN
M. T. Šajković

'My whole literary activity has embodied for me but one definite ideal value, but one aim, but one hope—and that I do not strive for fame or money, but only and solely for the synthesis of my imaginative and literary ideals.' Was it a philosopher or a preacher who wrote that? No, it was a novelist, for there are some novelists whose works will suffice to shorten a railway journey or to pass some minutes before we sleep, and there are others whose novels embody the deepest truth in a tale. Fyodor M. Dostoevsky, whose aim we have just quoted, was the second kind of novelist, for he was one of the great thinkers as well as one of the great story-tellers of his time, and Miriam T. Šajković has given us a fascinating book on him.[1]

Dostoevsky could write for others because he himself had passed through the deep waters. He knew years of continuous poverty; he knew ill-health, for he suffered from epilepsy. He knew sorrow, for his first wife died of tuberculosis and the first child of his second marriage died in infancy.

He could produce masterpieces under the lash of cruel necessity. He was in debt to the extent of three thousand roubles. In twenty-six days Dostoevsky produced *The Gambler*, 'a novel of seven folios'.

Dostoevsky knew men. He had what his friend Baron Vrangel called 'a superb humanity'. It was his Siberian exile which gave him his insight into men. For five years in Siberia he was herded with a crowd of exiles in a wooden hut, unbearably hot in summer, with ice three inches thick on the windows in winter, and with filth an inch deep on the floor. He was to write afterwards: 'To be alone is a natural need, like eating and drinking, for in that kind of concentrated communism one be-comes a whole-hearted enemy of mankind'.

Dostoevsky loved Jesus Christ. Of God he said: 'I love and I believe that I am loved', and therein he found peace. Of Jesus Christ he said that his creed was: 'I believe that there is nothing lovelier, deeper, more sympathetic, more rational, more manly, and more perfect than the Saviour'. He called the Incarnation, 'the visible apparition of the Beautiful'. He was never parted from his New Testament. He often used to open it at random and cast his eye on the left-hand page for guidance. His last illness began with a burst artery in one of his lungs through over-exertion in shifting his bookcase. He asked for his New Testament and his wife brought it to him. It opened at Mt 3¹⁴, Dostoevsky's eye fell on the saying of Jesus: 'Suffer it to be so now'. 'Do you see, Anya?' he said. ' "Suffer it to be so now", it means that I am to die.' He closed his book and so he died.

Dostoevsky was a lover of all things beautiful. When he was talking of the education of children, he said: 'Man should not step out of childhood into life without the embryo of something positive and beautiful; without these a generation should not be permitted to start on its life journey'.

From Moody the American evangelist to Dostoevsky, the Russian novelist and visionary is a big step. Barclay, however, with his customary versatility, makes it without difficulty. There is a self-revealing passage in this review 'Dostoevsky could write for

---

[1] Published by OUP.

others because he himself had passed through the deep waters'. There is an echo of the moving references, written years after this review, in Barclay's Testament of Faith *concerning the tragic loss of his own daughter. And there is more than an echo here, also, of the particular kind of suffering with which we have become sadly familiar in recent years as figures like Solzhenitsyn and other 'dissidents', who with their backgrounds of Siberian exile and labour camps, have emerged upon the Western scene. (See p. 103 below.)*

AFRICAN SAINT: THE STORY OF APOLO KIVEBULAYA
A. Luck

It is good for us sometimes to be reminded that the Acts of the Apostles is an unfinished story; and we are vividly reminded of that in this book.[1]

Apolo was the great African saint of the Church of Uganda, and he died as recently as 1933. He was a man 'obsessed by Jesus Christ'.

One of the most extraordinary things about him was that he was the apostle to the pygmies in the depths of the forests.

Like Paul, Apolo had more than once his definite visions of Christ. When he was in prison and while he was wondering how much longer he could endure physical torture and pain Jesus Christ appeared to him. 'I saw Jesus Christ like the sun, and He said to me: "Be of good cheer. I am with you". I answered and said: "Who is speaking to me?" He replied the second time saying: "I am Jesus Christ. Preach to My people. Do not be afraid."'

Whatever be the explanation, Apolo seemed to have a power not of this earth. 'He who appeared to me', he said, 'has given me grace in difficult languages.' In time of drought he prayed for rain. 'He will ever give you rain', he said. 'I prayed and it rained straight away, and in that way God made me do that as a miracle.' More than once his faith enabled him to heal the sick. He arrived in a place where a woman was suffering severe abdominal pain. The people asked him for medicines. 'I have no medicine', he said, 'but there is something I can do.' He prayed, gave the woman two cups of coffee, and she was cured.

We sometimes see in Apolo a man who re-enacted the ancient prophetic dramatic actions. In Mboga he took the sacred tribal drum, an object of the greatest superstitious veneration, and used it to summon the Christians to worship. Even the old gods were, so to speak, converted. In another place a cannibal was converted. He had worn round his neck a necklace made of small bones from his victims—a powerful charm. Apolo in the moment of baptism made him take it off and lay it aside for ever. The man had passed from the protection of the old gods into the possession of Jesus Christ.

Again and again we come on incidents which remind us of the New Testament Acts. We find Apolo in gaol converting his gaolers, as Paul did. We find the people coming and burning their charms, as the people of Ephesus did.

Apolo had three great gifts. First, he had a saintly humility. When a young teacher was unwilling to leave a large post for work in the forest, Apolo, then a Canon of the Church, asked that he might be allowed to go. Second, he had on him a happy radiance like the light of God. Third, above all he lived with Christ. 'When I was in the chain gang', he said, 'Jesus had hold of my hand.'

Mrs. Luck has told a great story simply and vividly and with full documentation. It is right that Apolo Kivebulaya's memory should be preserved.

Since the rule of Amin, Uganda has produced many tragic and heroic Christian martyrs, from the anglican Archbishop Luwum to a host of nameless and humble men and women who have been called upon to stand

[1] Published by SCM PRESS.

witness to their faith. This, which was written long before those events, reminds us of the rich vein of strong Christian faith which has been a feature of Ugandan Christianity since the great days of nineteenth century missionary enterprise. Here, in this story of a Ugandan who took it upon himself to be an apostle to the pygmies in the depths of the forests, Barclay takes note of a truly remarkable story. He nowhere expresses any doubts as to the credibility of the miraculous elements in the narrative, as when Apolo prays for rain, and rain comes. It is enough for Barclay to note that here is a book which returns to the atmosphere of the early Church as reflected in the Book of the Acts, and as he is ever-ready to remind us, merely continues the unfinished story of Jesus and his Church.

THE FAITH OF ROBERT BROWNING
Hugh Martin

It is unlikely that any student of A. J. Gossip will ever forget the name of Robert Browning. Dr. Martin tells of a friend's comment on a certain well-known minister: 'He's an old-fashioned type. You know; he quotes Browning in the pulpit'. But for all that it is unlikely that there will ever come a day when people will not read Robert Browning. Thirty years ago the first book on which I ever wrote a notice for THE EXPOSITORY TIMES was a study of the thought of Browning, and still the books come and still they are read.

When he liked, Browning was one of the great lyric poets, but also when he liked, he could be extremely obscure. He himself admitted the charge that his writing was too hard for many with whom he would have liked to communicate. 'I have never pretended', he said, 'to offer such literature as should be a substitute for a cigar or a game of dominoes to an idle man'. The trouble as Swinburne said of him was that 'he never thinks but at full speed'. Everyone remembers Tennyson's jest—he was a good friend of Browning for all that —when he said that in all 'Sordello' there were just two lines which he could understand, the first and the last, and that they were both untrue. The first is: 'Who will may hear Sordello's story told', and the last is: 'Who would has heard Sordello's story told'. Browning was certainly no saccharine singer, for he was seeker and singer in one.

Sometimes there was in Browning an oddly up-to-date character. He wrote 'Paracelsus' before he was twenty-three, an extraordinary performance, and he published it in 1835, long before Darwin and evolution had exploded on the Victorian scene, and there and in other poems Browning has curious fore-glimpses of the gospel of evolution':

For these things still upward,
    progress is
The law of life, man is not Man as
    yet.
... all tended to mankind,
And, man produced, all has its
    end thus far:
But in completed man begins
    anew
A tendency to God.

Believing as he did, Browning saw life above all in terms of *choice* and of *probation*. 'Life's business being just the terrible choice', he writes. Life for him is intolerable, 'If you bar me from assuming earth to be a pupil's place'. He talks of man,

Getting increase of knowledge,
    since he learns
Because he lives, which is to be
    a man.
For this reason a man ought to thank
God for temptation:
Temptation sharp? Thank God
    a second time!
Why comes temptation but for
    man to meet
And master and make crouch
    beneath his foot,
And so be pedestaled in
    triumph? Pray
'Lead us into no such
    temptation, Lord!'

This book[1] is easy to read, and it does introduce the reader to the best of Browning, and Browning was the poet who could make one of his characters say:

I say, the acknowledgement of
    God in Christ
Accepted by thy reason, solves
    for thee
All questions in the earth and
    out of it.

[1] Published by SCM PRESS, 1963.

It is rare to find among Barclay's reviews one which really dates, but this may be the exception. Perhaps Barclay knew of this when he quotes a comment of a certain preacher that 'he's an old fashioned type. . . . He quotes Browning in the pulpit'. That would certainly date a preacher today, if indeed such preacher could be found.

The verse, which is as convoluted as the thoughts of Browning and which had so strong an appeal to our forbears —William Temple, for example, was a great admirer—seems now to speak both of and from another world. Nevertheless Barclay, who was himself a student and then colleague of Gossip, cannot overlook a debt, from whatsoever source.

PARSON'S PITCH
David Sheppard

David Sheppard has had a kind of story-book life—captain of Cambridge, opening batsman for Sussex and England, young clergyman in Islington, and now Warden of the Mayflower Family Centre in Canning Town. He has told us about it all, modestly, movingly and charmingly in *Parson's Pitch.*[1]

David Sheppard was never very far away from the Church, but it was the preaching at Cambridge of a certain American Dr. Barnhouse which made him quite suddenly discover that Christianity meant more than being simply decent and good. His faith was and is a simple faith. He tells how late at night he walked back to his rooms in Trinity Hall sure that the most important thing in the world was that he should get right with God. 'Lord,' he prayed, 'I don't know where this is going to take me, but I'm willing to go with You. Please make me willing.'

There is nothing of the fanatic about David Sheppard. He has that wise tolerance which does enable him to get alongside all sorts of people. 'The tension of true education', he says with real insight, 'is to to hold decisive beliefs and at the same time to listen to others who think in another way, and to respect them.' And how well and how simply David Sheppard translates that into action in his own life! He tells how in one match a bowler set so deliberately defensive a field that scoring was almost impossible and the match in danger of being ruined. He protested violently and even angrily to the bowler and they had hot words. He got back to the pavilion and suddenly realized that that was no way for a Christian to behave. So he went into the other team's dressing-room and in front of the whole team publicly apologized for his words—and in so doing he made that bowler his friend for life. David Sheppard took his Christianity into his cricket with him.

His work in the Mayflower Family Centre in Canning Town has been a notable and a successful experiment, and he has certain wise things to say about such work.

Of course, the book is rich in cricket stories. Ramadhin the West Indian went for a rash run and David Sheppard threw down his wicket. Ramadhin said when he arrived back in the pavilion: 'Ramadhin he try to steal a run, and the Reverend he say, "Thou shalt not steal!"' We see Freddie Trueman looking round on the plane to see if David Sheppard had his clerical collar on, and seeing that he had, saying: 'We're all right, lads. The Rev's got his working overalls on.' And as a lightning ball from a fast bowler shot past his bat to be taken by the wicket-keeper there booms a voice: 'And it came to pass!'

England has always had a record of great Christian sportsmen whose ability in the field was used in the service of Jesus Christ and David Sheppard bids fair to rank high amongst them. As we read this book we can only say, 'Well played, Sir!' and may the innings continue a long time yet.

A good many things have happened to the writer of the book under review in the ten years since it first appeared. David Sheppard, now Bishop of Liverpool, and the author of a much weightier book than this, Built as a City, *a study of the urban challenge*

[1] Published by HODDER & STOUGHTON, 1966.

to the Church, has obviously matured considerably. Here Barclay is concerned with the David Sheppard of an earlier day when, as Warden of the Mayflower Family Centre in Canning Town, London, he was chiefly known to the public as a former test cricketer and Captain of England. Barclay concludes his piece with the words 'may the innings continue a long time yet'. It appears not only to be doing so; but also contributing considerably to the score.

ERNEST RENAN: A CRITICAL BIOGRAPHY
H. W. Wardman

A man who leaves behind him some forty octavo volumes of theology, moral and political philosophy, history, essays, drama, biography and autobiography has at least an excellent chance of leaving something which will last. Such a man was Ernest Renan, and his story is well told and his thought is well expounded by Dr. Wardman.[1]

He came of a humble Breton family; he was intended for the priesthood, but, not without a struggle, he was compelled to abandon it. 'Decision', he wrote to his sister, 'is a terrible word'. Catholicism he was later to say meant 'the cretinisation of the individual', and Renan was a man who had to be free to go his own way.

Renan was 'the Messiah of religious humanism'. He was intent upon 'the rational verification of Christianity'. He wanted a rational faith with all the miracle removed and all the legend reasonably interpreted. It was a human Jesus which he gave to men, a Jesus *si beau, si pur*, 'an eminent personality', 'an incomparable man'. There were many who called him a Judas, but the common people heard him gladly. His *Life of Jesus* was published in 1863 and in one year it had sold fifty thousand copies and had been translated into many different languages. And it is still a moving book to read. But it is to Renan the man that we must confine ourselves.

1. Renan was an intellectual aristocrat, and he knew it. Anger he despised, for it has to be shared. 'Disdain is a subtle and rare pleasure which can be kept to oneself; it is discreet because it is self-sufficient.' He speaks of 'the inertia, the herd of brutes', and in contrast of 'the aristocrats of the spirit', who must be 'the bastions of the spirit'. 'The function of the universities is to produce aristocrats . . . who will refuse to be the interpreters of the shallow thoughts of the herd.'

2. Yet this sense of superiority was in a real sense for service. There had to be identification. 'The man of superior gifts who seeks the good has always had to fall in with the weaknesses of people. Poor mankind! He who wants to serve it must get down to its level, speak its language. Superiority is a gift but it is a responsibility.

3. Renan knew that his function was to disturb. He could not stand the sight of men 'stagnating indulgently in their warm environment'. It was said of him in regard to the Roman Catholic Church: 'You have murdered sleep'. And it is something to stab a sleeping Church awake.

4. He had a curiously detached view of life, for all his enjoyment of it, and he was called 'the most jovial' exegete who ever taught. It is not without significance that he wrote a notable book on Ecclesiastes. He describes the life for which he thanked the Divine Cause as 'a charming stroll through reality'.

It would not be true to say that Dr. Wardman has written a sympathetic biography of Renan; his book is indeed critical; but we are indebted to him for bringing to life again a scholar who can never wholly be forgotten.

The uproar—and it is not too strong a word—created by Renan's La Vie de Jésus, *published in 1863, in which he repudiated the supernatural element in the life of Christ, seems a long way off from our world now. It*

[1] Published by THE ATHLONE PRESS, 1964.

*was enough, however, to lead to the
removal of Renan from his Chair of
Hebrew at the College of France. (Later
he was reinstated, and was eventually
appointed Director of the College under
the Third Republic.) Barclay
justly comments that Renan's Life of
Jesus is still a moving book to read. As
to the man himself, he notes carefully
the points about Renan's character made
by the author: that he was an intellectual
aristocrat, that he felt his function was
to disturb, and that his sense of
superiority was part of a desire to
serve the truth. To the contemporary
reader, who has lived through the
period characterized by Bultmann, Hans
Kung and Archbishop Lefebvre, the
persecution of Renan may well seem
surprising.*

MARKINGS
Dag Hammarskjöld

There is always a special interest when a distinguished man of affairs turns writer, and this is true of this book which consists of extracts from the journals of Dag Hammarskjöld, who was Secretary-General to the United Nations.[1]

At some time Mr. Hammarskjöld had an experience which altered his life. In 1952 he writes: 'What I ask is absurd: that life shall have a meaning. What I strive for is impossible: that my life shall acquire meaning'. But in 1961 he writes: 'Once I answered Yes to Someone— or Something. And from that hour I was certain that existence is meaningful and that, therefore, my life, in self-surrender, has a goal'.

Unquestionably he had the vision of sacrificial service.

The book is littered with epigrammatic sayings. 'Never look down to test the ground before taking your next step; only he who keeps his eye fixed on the far horizon will find the right road.' 'It is easy to be nice, even to an enemy—from lack of character.' 'Faith is God's marriage to the soul' 'To be humble is *not to make comparisons.*'

He had the grim gift of seeing himself. 'He stood erect—as a peg-top does so long as the whip keeps lashing it. He was modest—thanks to a robust conviction of his own superiority. He was unambitious— all he wanted was a life free from cares, and he took more pleasure in the failure of others than in his own successes. He saved his life by never risking it—and complained that he was misunderstood.' But that was written in 1941 before he said the great Yes.

As he saw himself, so he saw life. He saw life's danger. 'You cannot play with the animal in you without becoming wholly animal, play with falsehood without forfeiting your right to truth, play with cruelty without losing your sensitivity of mind. He who wants to keep his garden tidy, doesn't reserve a plot for weeds.' He saw life's destiny. 'To become free and responsible. For this alone was man created, and he who fails to take the Way which could have been his shall be lost eternally.'

There are times when he could pray:

'Give me a pure heart—that I
    may see Thee,
A humble heart—that I may
    hear Thee,
A heart of love—that I may
    serve Thee,
A heart of faith—that I may
    abide in Thee.'

Dag Hammarskjöld could say: 'In our age, the road to holiness necessarily passes through the world of action', but the strange thing about this book is that there is not a word about Suez or the Congo or any other great event in which its writer was involved.

On the whole this is a disappointing book. Dag Hammarskjöld to all intents and purposes arranged for its publication. Its words are the words of a private journal written for the world to read, and, therefore, the book is consistently self-conscious, and somehow the impression is left that the mind which is revealed just fails to be first class.

Here is a review which for once finds Barclay in condemnatory mood, and also quite possibly mistaken. Markings, by the enigmatic Swedish Secretary-General to the United Nations who was

[1] Published by FABER AND FABER, 1964.

killed in an air crash in Africa, is still well thought of, and his book made a considerable impact. But Barclay clearly does not like it, finding it disappointing. Even so, we can admire the author as a seeker after truth and his death, like his life, was heroic. He was on a peace mission when his aircraft crashed in the African bush; the question of foul-play in this tragedy has never been satisfactorily answered. But, whatever the verdict, Hammarskjöld died in the pursuit of peace, which was for him an article of faith.

TEILHARD DE CHARDIN: A BIOGRAPHICAL STUDY
C. Cuénot

It is a long time now since Callimachus remarked succinctly and devastatingly *mega biblion, mega kakon*, or, as we might paraphrase it, The bigger the book, the worse it is! Claude Cuénot's book[1] runs to 492 pages, but in this case it can truthfully be said that there is not a page too much. It is true that just as much space is given to Teilhard the scientist as to Teilhard the Christian thinker, and there is much of this book through which the general reader will have to toil, or which he may very legitimately 'skip', but a man of so many facets needed a book of so great a size.

Here is a picture of Teilhard the man. He was born an aristocrat. But for this Jesuit Father in France, in England, in China, in Africa, in America, life was indeed 'an endless pilgrimage', and that with the sorrow of being at least partly exiled from his beloved France by his still more beloved Church.

The book is scattered with tributes to Teilhard, all the more impressive because they come, as it were, in the passing. André Reymond who shared an expedition with him describes him, 'vibrant as a flag fluttering under the Asian sky, energetic, lively, generous, tireless, greeting each day with a burst of joyous enthusiasm'. And yet there was an aloofness too. Dr. George B. Barbour said of him: 'He was the noblest man I ever lived with'. De Terra said of him: 'He was the most cherished and revered human being I ever met'.

Teilhard had his aims. He had a sense of urgency. He did not die until 1955, but even in 1932 he was saying: 'I feel that I must hurry. I keep having the strong feeling that my sun is hastening towards its setting. It is four o'clock in the afternoon for me, so to speak'. His Church would never allow the publication of his writings during his lifetime—except the scientific ones. The checks he received, he says, awakened in him a new desire, to liberate. For him work was worship, and he said himself that for him research and adoration were one and the same thing.

But his great aim can be summed up in one new and strange word. He wanted to *Christify* everything. Life must be Christified, until every action is full of Christ, in the factory as in the monastery. Evolution must be Christified until it is seen as cosmogenesis, evolution in and to God. Evolution for him was convergent—not divergent—towards a final unity. That unity is of a spiritual nature, but it involves not the destruction but the transformation, sublimation, climax of matter. Teilhard was at one and the same time in the first rank of the scientists and the mystics.

The orthodox leaders of his Church suspected him, and limited severely both his teaching and his writing. He was too big a man to rebel, but once the edge of the curtain lifted and he said to Père Bergounioux as he was leaving him: 'Pray for me, that I may not die embittered'. Teilhard will speak to the years to come when the little men who tried to silence him will have passed into oblivion.

This is a great biography of a great man.

It remains to be seen whether the Jesuit thinker and, in some sense,

[1] Published by BURNS AND OATES, 1965.

35

mystic who was Teilhard de Chardin, will ultimately receive a favourable verdict from history or not. Some still see in him a significant reconciler of science and religion, while others consider him to have been over-rated, and his message too obscure. His own church authorities, or at any rate the more orthodox among them, were suspicious of him. But Barclay seems to be in no doubt. 'This is a great biography', he says, 'of a great man'. Undoubtedly for Barclay, Teilhard's particular greatness lay more in the position of Christ he found for his system, than in the system itself.

JOSEPH PRIESTLEY: ADVENTURER IN SCIENCE AND CHAMPION OF TRUTH
F. W. Gibbs

There were in previous generations an expansiveness, an inclusiveness, and a catholicity in scholarship which seldom exist today in an age of specialism. Dr. Gibbs has given us an excellent biography of one of the great scientific and religious figures of the eighteenth century.[1]

Priestley was born in 1733. He was brought up to a meticulous honesty. He would in any event have been a tremendous toiler. 'Human happiness', he wrote, 'depends chiefly upon having some object to pursue, and upon the vigour with which our faculties are exerted in the pursuit.' But it may well be that the circumstances of his early life, as it were, drove him to scholarship. By the time he was in his early twenties, of the ancient languages he knew Latin, Greek, Hebrew, Chaldee, and Syriac, and of the modern languages French, German, and Italian. He had studied and read history, theology, and philosophy, and, of course, mathematics and science. He was to become one of the greatest experimenters of his day in the realms of chemistry and electricity, and for a very large part of the time he was serving as the pastor of some dissenting chapel at the same time as he did his scientific work. To all his other accomplishments he added a knowledge of shorthand.

Priestley was an experimenter rather than a constructor and he knew it. He excelled rather at observation than at interpretation. He certainly repeatedly pointed the way for others to follow. His work was done in three areas.

1. He was a scientist. This book is so written that the scientific part of Priestley's life is dealt with in certain self-contained chapters. These chapters are very readable, but the reader can, if he so wishes, omit them. From the scientific part we learn that Priestley was the inventor of aerated water!

2. He was a theologian. It is here that he ran into real trouble, for he was by conviction a Unitarian. In the ancient world dead men tended to be worshipped by the idolaters, and that happened to Jesus. He insisted that the only guide is reason. 'Have nothing to do with a parliamentary religion, or a parliamentary God.' Strong meat!

3. He was a political theorist. He was a pacifist; he thought the possession of colonies an intolerable thing. Kings there might be, but only in their proper place, and magistrates are no more than the servants of the people. It is not insignificant that the French revolutionaries made Joseph Priestley, Thomas Paine, Jeremy Bentham, William Wilberforce, and George Washington honorary citizens of France. It was of the explosive power of ideas that Priestley spoke, but his enemies took it literally, and Priestly ended his days an exile in the new colony of America, a man for whom there was no safety in England.

Dr. Gibbs has produced a sober yet fascinating biography of a most extraordinary man.

This was a book about a man who was not only remarkable but also singularly versatile. The like of Priestley, just as the like of a not wholly dissimilar figure, Benjamin Franklin is not, as Barclay points out, to be found nowadays. Specialization

[1] Published by NELSON & CO., 1965.

too often means the end of versatility. Priestley was a great polymath: scientist, theologian, political theorist and ardent democrat. Along with Thomas Paine, Jeremy Bentham, William Wilberforce and George Washington, he was made an honorary citizen of revolutionary France. He was also a Unitarian, an apostle of reason as a guide to conduct, and a victim of an ignorant mob who wrecked and destroyed the priceless library at his Birmingham home. As Barclay rightly says, 'a most extraordinary man'.

I KNEW DIETRICH BONHOEFFER
W. D. Zimmerman and R. Gregor Smith (Eds.)
(E.T. by K. Gregor Smith)

A martyr has always a right to be heard. That is why this is so fascinating a book.[1] The book consists of memories of Bonhoeffer contributed by more than thirty people, and covering his whole life from his childhood to his death.

In this volume Bonhoeffer emerges as a combination of paradoxes.

(i) He was a man of discipline who yet loved the good things of life. *Zucht*, discipline, was a word that Bonhoeffer loved, and yet as one of his friends says, 'He loved to eat well'. And another friend tells how on a visit to Geneva his then shabby wardrobe was replaced by new things. 'I never had', she says, 'such a joyful and grateful customer.' He was the ascetic who enjoyed life.

(ii) He cared intensely and yet he was detached. 'To keep a distance in manners and spirit, without being cool, to be interested without curiosity—that was about his line.' 'He liked to keep his distance, and he did not permit any undue familiarity.' He astonished a friend by telling him that, apart from his relatives, he called only one person *du*. And another says of him: 'With people, he was as ready to listen as to speak, to identify as to analyse, to participate as to investigate'.

(iii) He was accurate and yet a believer in the power of the dream. Of his teaching, one who studied with him said: 'What was far more important for us was to find straight ways of thinking, and to learn not to slink off into side issues, or to be satisfied with premature cheap answers'. And yet he could also say: 'An author should not be attacked or interpreted from one of his negative sentences: we should ask what he intends to say with the whole book'. He approved the view that 'literature was there to make men dream'. He

was the servant but not the slave of accuracy.

(iv) He was the theologian but he was also the man of action. 'He willed what he thought.' For the Church to have nothing to do with politics was for the Church to capitulate to politics. 'If', he said, 'a drunken driver is at the wheel, it is not just the minister's job to comfort the relations of those he has killed, but if possible to seize the steering-wheel.' That is why he believed that secular freedom is also worth dying for.

Above all there were three driving forces in his life. There was the conviction of the right.

'If we claim to be Christians', he said, 'there is no room for expediency.' There was the sense of destiny. He might well have stayed safe out of Germany; he went back. 'I know what I have chosen', he said. Supremely he was a man of faith. As he walked out to die on 5th April 1945, he whispered to a fellow-prisoner: 'This is the end. But for me it is the beginning of life'. As Hellmut Traub said of Bonhoeffer's book on ethics: 'He has been granted to live and to die it'.

It can be said of this book that it is worthy of its subject—and praise cannot be higher.

'He being dead yet speaks', may well be said of the subject of this book and of this review. The memory of Bonhoeffer, 'that fascinating man', as a British military doctor who saw him immediately before his execution described him, seems to have grown

[1] Published by WM. COLLINS & SONS.

stronger rather than diminished with time. His hanging by the Gestapo in the April of 1945 seems still to be a shadow upon the collective consciousness of civilization. Books about him abound, for example, by Mary Bosanquet as well as the fuller and deeper studies from his own native Germany. What Bonhoeffer might have given to the world, could he but have escaped the rope in 1945 will always be a sad and unanswerable question.

AUGUSTINE OF HIPPO
Peter Brown

A book which runs to almost 160,000 words and which has a bibliography listing more than 350 volumes or articles is by any standard a big book.[1] Not only is this a big book in size, it is also a great book. In it there appears before us in all the panorama of his life and thought one of the greatest figures in the Church. In spite of the length the interest never flags and few biographers can ever have got so near the heart of their subject as Peter Brown has.

Long before he was a bishop Augustine was a rhetorician and a philosopher, and to the end he knew the magic of words. He spoke of 'words, these precious cups of meaning'. He spoke of an argument as 'dragging vivid thoughts through the long, twisting lanes of speech'. There was in him a sheer romanticism and a love of the dramatic. In his youth he loved the theatre, especially scenes which told of the parting of lovers. 'I went out of my way', he said, 'to find something to make me weep.' 'I was not yet in love', he said of his youth, 'but I was in love with love . . . What I needed most was to love and be loved.'

However hard he tried not to be, Augustine could never have been anything but a scholar. 'Give me, O Lord, to know and understand', he prayed. 'God has given me a mind to place the Discovery of Truth above all things, to wish for nothing else, to think of nothing else, to love nothing else.' 'At that time, there was no one more open to being taught than I was.'

Knowledge came by many ways. 'It is yearning that makes the heart deep.' Discussion is good. 'Really great things, when discussed by little men, can usually make such men grow big.' But to the intellectual search there must be added feeling.

He does not say of a book which was an epoch in his life, 'It changed my views'; he says, 'It changed my way of feeling'.

A man like this was bound to be a great preacher. He had a supreme sensitivity for entering into the minds and hearts of his hearers. 'An audience will identify itself only with an excited man; and Augustine would be excited for them.' His one idea was 'to break the bread' of Scripture and 'to feed' the multitude. 'I am the servant, the bringer of food, not the master of the house. I lay out before you that from which I also draw my life.'

Augustine was the great phrasemaker. He spoke of the human race as 'the great invalid'. He spoke of the mind as 'ready to lie down' for weariness. He spoke of 'the sweet task of sinning'. 'The Devil', he said, 'is not to be blamed for everything; there are times when a man is his own devil.'

We have done far less than justice to this book. It will unquestionably rank as one of the great biographies. It is the most erudite of books, and meticulously documented, and yet astonishingly easy to read. All that one can say of it is that it is a book which in its learning and its love is worthy of its subject.

To review a book of this size in an article of this length would be a major challenge for anyone. It is therefore all the more fortunate that the task fell to Barclay, although even he is constrained to say that he has done 'far less than justice to this book.' How

[1] Published by FABER AND FABER, 1967; p/b ed. 1969.

could it be otherwise? Here, nonetheless, are colourful and memorable details about the great Augustine which help to humanize the scholar and theologian and which, in their selection, are typical of Barclay, who quotes with obvious satisfaction 'really great things, when discussed by little men, can usually make such men grow big'. And it is good to be reminded that it was Augustine of all people who said, that 'the Devil is not to be blamed for everything; there are times when a man is his own Devil'.

READINGS FROM POPE JOHN
V. A. Yzermans

Vincent A. Yzermans has done us a service in compiling a brief selection from Pope John's writings.[1] There are some men of whom it may be said that after their stay in it the world can never be quite the same again—and that was true of Pope John.

Mr. Yzermans' book begins with a picture of Pope John on the opening night of the Second Vatican Council. 'Pope John XXIII stood in the window of his private study, smiling at thousands and thousands of cheering Romans below in St. Peter's Square. He quietened them. He spoke to them. "Go home", he said, "and make love grow from here to everywhere".' It is not, Mr. Yzermans thinks, too much to say: 'There was a man sent from God whose name was John'.

Mr. Yzermans picks out certain characteristics of the mind and heart of Pope John. First, he 'was almost obsessed with the importance of the I–Thou relationship'. 'He rekindled the fires of Christian love in our hearts because he himself was aflame with God's love.' Second, he was convinced that the Eucharist ought to be 'the bond of love and unity among God's people'. 'The holy Eucharist, will it or not, fills all of us with an ecumenical desire.' Third, he was a man of irrepressible joy. He knew the pessimism of the world. 'We note', he said 'that there is a kind of lamentation rising from practically all contemporary literature.' He closes an address to the Italian farmers: 'We offer the Lord a prayer, on behalf of you all, for your families and your work so that joy in the Lord may always sing in your hearts'.

For him the truth was as sacred as love. A man, he said, has a fourfold duty to the truth—to think it, to honour it, to speak it and to do it.

The truth for him was not static. His was the adventurous mind.

He could challenge the Christian with the conviction that every Christian must be an ambassador for Christ. Twice he quotes a great passage from one of Chrysostom's *Homilies:* 'Christ left us on earth in order that we should become like beacons of light and teachers unto others.

Pope John was never afraid to recall men to the great central issues, and often he does so in the words of the great fathers of the Church. 'While human society is being carried along to a new order', he writes, 'far-reaching tasks remain for the Church; as we have learned, this has been the case in every period of great distress. The Church is now called upon to take the perennial, vital power of the Gospel and inject it into the veins of human society today, which glories in its recent scientific and technological advances, at the same time that it is suffering damage to its social order, which some people have tried to repair without God's assistance.'

To read this book is to see the basic Christian faith applied to the problems of life and living. It may be that the more fanatical of the so-called Protestants will not like us to say so, but this book has in it the apostolic accent.

Many years have passed since the brief, but epoch-making papacy of the octagenarian John XXIII. The fact that his initiatives have led to lasting changes in the Roman Catholic Church becomes increasingly apparent. It is never

[1] Published by A. R. MOWBRAY & CO., 1968.

to be forgotten that Vatican II, from which so many developments have sprung, would not have been but for this remarkable Pope. Barclay's review of a selection from his works, together with one writer's comments on the man himself, is thus of continuing interest. It is characteristic of Barclay that he can write as sympathetically and with such obvious pleasure of a great Pope, as he can of John Knox (see p.7 above) or Martin Luther (see p.53 below).

THE ESSENCE OF T. H. HUXLEY
C. Bibby

There are few greater functions that a man can fulfil than the function of acting as an introducer to greatness. Cyril Bibby introduces us to one of the greatest men of his generation. The book consists almost entirely of extracts from Huxley's writings, but each section is prefaced by a short, but vivid, introduction.[1]

Huxley had no more than two years schooling, but no more erudite man ever lived, and no man ever did more for science, the more so because his erudition was uniquely allied to a genius for teaching ordinary people.

Few men have added a new word to the English language, but Huxley did, the word *agnostic*. He could not call himself an atheist, a theist, a pantheist, a materialist, an idealist, a Christian. He plead with people, even with scientists, to learn the art of arts, the art of saying: 'I don't know'. Suspended judgment he called 'that most wholesome state of mind'. It was neither cynicism nor despair; it was humility, which made him take this title to himself.

Huxley valued disagreement. 'There is', he said, 'no more effectual method of clearing up one's own mind on any subject than by talking it over, so to speak, with men of real power and grasp, who have considered it from a totally different point of view.' Scientific jargon was as anathema to him as religious jargon was.

He was greatest of all when he wrote on education. 'That man', he writes, 'has, I think, had a liberal education who has been so trained in youth that his body is the ready servant of his will, and does with ease and pleasure all the work that, as a mechanism, it is capable of; whose intellect is a clear, cold, logical engine, with all its parts of equal strength, and in smooth working order; ready, like a steam engine, to be turned to any kind of work, and spin the gossamers as well as forge the anchors of the mind; whose mind is stored with a knowledge of the great and fundamental truths of Nature and of the laws of her operations; one who, no stunted ascetic, is full of life and fire, but whose passions are trained to come to heel by a vigorous will, the servant of a tender conscience; who has learned to love all beauty, whether of Nature or of art, to hate all vileness, and to respect others as himself.' No nobler educational ideal was ever set down.

Huxley's writings are scattered with aphorisms. 'History warns us ... that it is the customary fate of new truths to begin as heresies and to end as superstitions.' 'If individuality has no play, society does not advance; if individuality breaks out of all bounds, society perishes.' 'Their tolerance is large because their belief is small.' 'Science is, I believe, nothing but *trained and organised common sense*.' He once said that the way to die was in the middle of an unfinished article—and he did die correcting his proofs.

We owe Professor Bibby a very large debt for introducing us to the thought of a supremely great, and still a supremely relevant, thinker.

Huxley was one of the central figures in the great science-versus-religion controversy of the nineteenth century. Drawing our attention to this book of extracts from his writings, Barclay does a valuable service in reminding us that Huxley was also by any standards, and in any context, a great man. At this distance of time it

[1] Published by MACMILLAN & CO., 1968.

45

is astonishing to realize that in Huxley's own day so many people were prepared to condemn him. Barclay, however, is only too eager to recognize his greatness and he clearly takes pleasure in passing on some of the wise words which the writer of this book has gathered together. Thus Huxley called suspended judgment 'that most wholesome state of mind'. Barclay is similarly endued with such humility. And, to one of such unremitting literary industry as Barclay himself, one remark of Huxley must have had particular appeal: 'He once said that the way to die was in the middle of an unfinished article—and he did die correcting his proofs'.

ONCE CAUGHT, NO ESCAPE
Norman Grubb

No books are so interesting as autobiographies, especially when they are honest revelations of a man's life and thoughts and beliefs.

Norman Grubb is a very considerable figure in the missionary world. He was a colleague of C. T. Studd—he is married to Studd's daughter—and he was and is the great apostle of what is commonly called the Faith—Mission type of work. In one sense nothing could be further from the truth than this book's view of the Christian faith and the Christian duty.[1]

There is the identification of Christianity with the doing and not doing of certain things. 'So on Armistice Day,' Norman Grubb writes, 'as the victory sirens were sounding, I threw my tobacco pouch into a ploughed field and that was the last of it.'

There is the not unusual conservative intolerance. During Norman Grubb's university days after the First World War there was some talk about co-operation between the religious societies. There was a meeting with the representatives of S.C.M. 'After an hour's talk, I asked Rolloe point-blank, "Does the S.C.M. put the atoning blood of Jesus Christ central?" He hesitated and then said, "Well, we acknowledge it, but not necessarily central". Dan Dick and I then said that this settled the matter for the C.I.C.C.U. We could never join something that did not maintain the atoning blood of Jesus Christ as its centre; and we parted company.'

There is the not seldom found contempt for and suspicion of scholarship. Norman Grubb tells of the Bible study groups he ran. 'I have never used commentaries, or very rarely. I have always felt it was better that I should get what was original to me, even if it was thin

material.' He is a reckless man who deliberately despoils himself of the wealth of men's minds in biblical study.

There is a view of prayer which is not really Christian. He talks about praying students 'who kept not silence and gave God no rest', as if God could be prodded or badgered into action.

There is the Faith-Mission principle that God is trusted for everything. There are no salaries; there is no financial preparation for a project. What is prayed for will arrive and God will provide. Where did the money come from and where does it come from? From people who have lived thoughtful, careful and well-planned lives. The whole flaw in this view of life is that it demands that certain people must be responsible in order that others may be supremely irresponsible. Some must live by prudence in order to allow others to live by faith.

Norman Grubb knows well, as he finely says, that 'the diamond of God's truth has just too many sparkling facets for any one pair of eyes'. He may not have used commentaries but his devotional reading has been wide and choice. John of the Cross, Teresa, Eckhart and many another, not least Kierkegaard. And whatever else is true, Norman Grubb is right when he says that the work of himself and his colleagues has always been founded on the four pillars—sacrifice, faith, holiness and fellowship.

Here we find Barclay faced with a task of writing about a book which

[1] Published by LUTTERWORTH PRESS, 1969.

he quite clearly disliked. He is careful, nonetheless, to do justice to the stature of Norman Grubb, in his day a notable figure on the missionary scene. Barclay attributes to his work the fact that it was founded upon sacrifice, faith, holiness and fellowship. But that said, he has to note that here is a man who identified Christianity with the doing and not doing of certain non-moral things; who was intolerant; who had a suspicion of scholarship, especially Bible study; and who lived by the principle of leaving to God the settlement of his material affairs. Barclay's comment on this last point is unusually ironic: 'some must live by prudence in order to allow others to live by faith'. But it must not be surmised that Barclay was against such practices per se. (In his review of St. Francis, p. 65 below, he highlights this same principle). It is more the unthinking generalisations about this which he castigates, and the harmful infliction of them on others.

WILLIAM TYNDALE
C. H. Williams

It is a simple matter of fact that every 'official' translation of the New Testament down to the New English Bible was nothing other than a revision of Tyndale. Tyndale was Coverdale's main source. The Bishops' Bible was a revision of the Great Bible, which was the work of Coverdale. The translators of the Authorized Version had as their deliberate policy to depart as little as possible from the Bishops' Bible. The Revised Version translators were tied to the language of the Authorized Version, even in the cases where they made changes. The aim of the Revised Standard Version was to maintain the Tyndale-King James tradition. From the 1520's to the 1950's Tyndale has dominated the New Testament in English. In this book we are presented with an excellent summary of Tyndale's life and work.[1]

There are some interesting background facts. At the beginning of the sixteenth century the population of England and Wales was about 3,000,000. Sir Thomas More thought that four out of every ten could not read; Stephen Gardiner thought that only a hundredth of the population could read. Nonetheless between 1525 and 1528 something like 8,000 copies of Tyndale's translation were printed. It may well be that Tyndale was one of the moving forces in producing a reading population. Tyndale was a man of clearly marked characteristics.

He was a really great scholar. Buschius visited Worms in 1526 and came back with news of an Englishman who had translated the New Testament, and who spoke seven languages like a native. He was meticulously accurate: 'I never altered one syllable of God's word against my conscience, nor would this day, if all that is in the earth, whether it might be pleasure, honour, or riches, might be given me'.

He was a realist. He discovered and faced the fact that 'there was no room in my lord of London's palace to translate the New Testament, but that there was no place to do it in all England'. He was open-eyed about people. For a time he had William Roy as an assistant. But he said of him: 'As long as he had no money, somewhat I could rule him; but as soon as he had gotten money he became like himself again'—and he was a 'crafty' man.

He had dauntless courage. 'In burning the New Testament they did none other than I looked for; no more shall they do, if they burn me also.' He expected a like courage from others, even if it meant the loss of everything. He writes to Frith, when Frith's life was in danger: 'Sir, your wife is well content with the will of God, and would not, for her sake, have the glory of God hindered'.

Not only is Tyndale the translator dealt with in this book. There are excellent chapters on Tyndale as a propagandist, a controversialist, a theologian and a political thinker.

This is a work of first-class scholarship written in the most interesting way, a book which all lovers of the English New Testament must read.

Despite the proliferation of translations and translators, Tyndale must remain a towering, indeed, a formative influence in the translation of the New Testament into English. He also stands as an heroic figure: 'In burning the New

[1] Published by NELSON & CO., 1969.

Testament', he said of his enemies, 'they did none other than I looked for; no more shall they do, if they burn me also'. And so, indeed, they did.

JOHN BUNYAN
R. L. Greaves

A book about a fascinating subject has every chance of being a fascinating book. No one can deny that John Bunyan is a fascinating subject and Richard L. Greaves has produced a fascinating book about him. The book is a volume in the Courtenay Studies in Reformation Theology.[1] It is not about John Bunyan's life; it is about his theology, and is all the more valuable for that.

John Bunyan is a study in paradoxes, and it is at some of these paradoxes that we will look. Bunyan was not a systematic theologian: 'the love of God is better felt and enjoyed, then talked of'.

The first of the paradoxes is that Bunyan had an awesome sense of the justice and the wrath of God and an equally passionate awareness of the grace and the love of God. The wrath of God is the execution of divine justice. Upon unrepentant sinners 'the wrath of God shall smoke to their eternal ruine'.

And yet God is unfathomable love. 'God is love; might some say, and Justice too: but his Justice is turned with Wisdom, Power, Holiness, and Truth, to love, yea, to love those that are found in his Son.'

The wrath turned to love through Jesus Christ, 'from whom, by whom, or through whom the Grace of God doth come to us'. Christ is 'the inlet to saving grace'. If any one ever taught a substitutionary atonement Bunyan did.

The second of the paradoxes is the paradox of God's call and man's answer. Bunyan believed completely in predestination, and his choice was before the creation of the world. God has the 'Prerogative Royal, without prejudice to them that are damned, to chuse and refuse at pleasure'. Further, that choice and grace are irrevocable. 'All the sins they commit, and all the judgments they deserve, cannot drive them out of the World before Conversion.' There is no such thing as free-will. 'I am not a Free-willer', said Bunyan. 'I abhor it.'

And yet this same Bunyan could plead with his people: 'Take heed, sirs, break off your sins'. 'Come to God in the name of the Son . . . and beg faith of him.' The two are put together as Paul might have put it: 'Get thy Will tipt with the heavenly grace . . . and then thou goest full speed for heaven'.

The third of the paradoxes is freedom and discipline. Bunyan believed in freedom, the freedom to worship, the freedom to be a gathered people. He so much believed in freedom that he would not agree that Baptism is a necessity.

But freedom which threatened the unity of the fellowship had to be mercilessly rooted out. The weeds must be pulled out of God's garden.

This is a meticulously documented and magnificently scholarly book. But the sheer interest of it never flags from beginning to end. It is an exceptionally beautifully produced book, a joy to handle and to read. Professor Greaves and his publishers have done a first-rate job.

If it is rare to find Barclay writing a harsh review, it is even rarer to find him producing one which gives evidence of either haste or fatigue or both. Perhaps this is an instance of that rarity, with the adjective 'fascinating' occurring four times in the first four lines, and the word 'paradox' twice in the first two lines of the second

[1] Published by THE SUTTON COURTENAY PRESS, 1969.

51

paragraph. However, even Homer can nod, and even Barclay has his off days. And yet none of this prevents him from writing well on the subject of Bunyan, or failing to note the paradoxes in his theology, such as that God's justice and wrath can co-exist with God's grace and love, or that an ardent belief in freedom could co-exist with religious intolerance. Barclay's ability to hold together apparently contradicting truths is an important aspect of thought, not the least aspect of which is its continuous assertion of the basic truths of the Gospel alongside his deep commitment to Biblical criticism and learning.

LUTHER: AN INTRODUCTION TO HIS THOUGHT
G. Ebeling

There is always an attraction in a personality in which there is an element of recklessness. When a man thinks adventurously and speaks vividly, other men will always listen to him. Such was Martin Luther, and Gerhard Ebeling has written a magnificent book about him.[1] The translation is by R. A. Wilson, and is so good that one would not know that one was reading a translation. The book is one which the non-expert can read with interest and with profit.

It is not a biography of Luther. It is an attempt—and an entirely successful attempt—to penetrate to 'the inner dynamics' of Luther's thought.

Apart altogether from his ability as a theologian Luther was a master of words, and the creator of the German language. Herder said of him: 'It is he who awoke and set free the sleeping giant of the German language'. Erasmus said of him that he brought Latin literature to an end.

He was one of the great Bible translators. He tells us that for three or even four weeks they would search how to express the meaning of one word. 'Sometimes we scarcely succeeded in finishing three lines in four days.' In an age when allegory ran riot he could say: 'Our first concern will be for the grammatical meaning, for this is the truly theological meaning'. He was determined to put Scripture into the language of the common people.

Humility was the very keynote of his nature both in the face of men and of God. He hated the very idea that any man should call himself a 'Lutheran'. This humility was the very basis of his religion. That is why the discovery of justification by faith was like the opening of the gates of paradise, because it was God who did it all.

But this humility was not weakness. When it came to a matter of principle he could say: 'In this matter I am prepared to be stubborn, blinkered and obstinate, and am glad to be called such, for here the thing is never to yield'.

He distrusted human reason and philosophy. He could speak about the 'putrid philosophers'. He could say: 'Reason is the Devil's whore, and can do nothing but shame and disgrace everything which God says and does'. Speculative theology belongs 'in hell with the Devil'.

This did not stop him being a prodigious worker. The Weimar edition of his works consists at present of one hundred folio volumes of about seven hundred pages each and the end is not yet in sight. Of his sermons two thousand are extant and of his letters two thousand eight hundred.

We have space to quote only two more things. One is Luther's very valuable principle for the use of Scripture. Scripture is the only standard for theological doctrine—*sola scriptura*. But, as the proverb has it, 'Scripture has a wax nose', that is to say, a man is apt to use Scripture as he wishes. Therefore, the standard for theological belief is not simply Scripture, it is *all* Scripture, *tota scriptura*. It is not single texts, but the whole of Scripture which are the test. The other thing is Luther's saying: 'To seek God outside Jesus is the Devil'. For Luther Jesus was the beginning, the middle and the end.

Martin Luther, bright star of the Reformation, has of recent years seemed to shine even more brightly as further

[1] Published by WM. COLLINS & SONS, 1972.

understandings of his complex character have emerged. Osborne's celebrated play is a case in point. Here is a figure who clearly has great attraction for Barclay. Luther was among other things, one of the great Bible translators. He was also a prodigious worker, who has left no less than one hundred volumes of seven hundred pages each, and that in an edition which is not as yet complete. Here again there are characteristics reminiscent of Barclay himself: a high view of Scripture; great humility before it; a commitment to the totality of the sacred page and, withal, an untiring application to serve it, and by it, God's people.

GEORGE WHITEFIELD: THE LIFE AND TIMES OF THE GREAT EVANGELIST OF THE EIGHTEENTH CENTURY REVIVAL

A. Dallimore

Some books are a man's life work; and such is this book by Arnold Dallimore.[1] This volume takes Whitefield's life from his birth in 1714 to his second visit to America in 1739–1740, and consists of 589 pages!

Of Whitefield as a preacher J. C. Ryle wrote: 'No Englishman, I believe, dead or alive, has ever equalled him'. The numbers who came to hear him preach are, even allowing for exaggeration, almost incredible. In Bristol at the Bowling Green at 6 a.m. on a Sunday morning he had more than 7,000. At Rose Green he had 20,000, and in the afternoon 23,000; in Moorfields in London 60,000; 'at a place called Mayfair, near Hyde Park Corner' 80,000.

In the eighteenth century in England religion was at a low ebb. When Queen Caroline was dying, some were surprised that none was called to pray with her. Robert Walpole the Prime Minister suggested to Princess Emma that the Archbishop of Canterbury be summoned. She hesitated and he said cynically: 'Pray, Madam, let this farce be played; the archbishop will act it very well. You may bid him be as short as you will. It will do the Queen no hurt, no more than any good; and it will satisfy all the good and wise fools, who will call us atheists if we don't profess to be as great fools as they are'.

Whitefield came like the voice of God. From one end of the social scale to the other they listened to him. The Bristol miners listened with their tears making furrows of white down the coal dust of their cheeks. Sarah, Duchess of Marlborough listened: 'God knows we all need mending, and none more than myself'. The children listened. A child heard him and became ill. 'I will go to Mr. Whitefield's God', he said before he died.

As a preacher he was supreme. He was blessed with a voice, which, Benjamin Franklin said, gave 'a pleasure of much the same kind with that received from an excellent piece of music'. He prayed for 'holy guile' to catch his hearers. He was in the end completely ecumenical: 'My sole question is "Are you a Christian?" '

He was the humblest of men despite his fame. He would never form a denomination. 'Let the name of Whitefield perish,' he said, 'but Christ be glorified.' Wesley once found fault with him, and he wrote in return: 'I thank you most heartily for your kind rebuke. I can only say it was most tender. I beseech you, whenever you see me doing wrong, rebuke me sharply'.

It is impossible to do justice to this massive book in a brief notice. It is not only a biography of Whitefield; it is genuinely a history of his life and times and not least a revaluation of John Wesley. Once in Georgia Whitefield prayed: 'God give me a deep humility, a well-guided zeal, a burning love and single eye, and then let men or devils do their worst'. This biography does justice to a man who prayed like that.

To review a book which, as Barclay claims for this one, was a man's life's work is a heavy responsibility. It is one which, however, Barclay clearly takes on all the more

[1] Published by BANNER OF TRUTH, 1970.

gladly because he feels that he can praise the book so warmly. (*No one, it may be observed, has ever seemed to solve the problem of how Whitefield, huge though his voice was, ever succeeded in making himself heard*). But Barclay's final praise for the book is that it does justice to a man great enough to have prayed, as once Whitefield did in Georgia: 'God give me a deep humility, a well guided zeal, a burning love and single eye, and then let men or devils do their worst'. Barclay, likewise, despite criticism and misunderstanding, is content to do his work and leave it to God.

MARTIN LUTHER KING
K. Slack

The voices of martyrs speak for all the world to hear, and Martin Luther King was a martyr. His story had been told simply and vividly and meaningfully by Kenneth Slack.[1]

Martin Luther King did not come from the poor and the oppressed classes. The place in which he was brought up in Atlanta in Georgia may have been in one sense a ghetto, but it was a very affluent ghetto. He had a first-class education, finishing up as a doctoral student in Boston.

His grandfather and his father were ministers of Ebenezer Baptist Church in Atlanta, and in his father's day that church had four thousand members. As he listened to his famous son preaching in St. Paul's in London he was heard to whisper: 'Make it plain, son, make it plain'.

In a sense the young Martin Luther King was as much against his own background as he was against the white man. His background was basically bourgeois. The negroes amongst whom he lived were wealthy; they worshipped success; they were far more interested in civil rights for themselves than they were in the human rights of their poorer brothers. Martin Luther King was much more practical. 'I am not concerned', he said, 'with the temperature of hell or the furnishings of heaven, but with the things men do here on earth.' 'There are still too many negro churches', he said, 'that are so absorbed in a good "over yonder" that they condition their members to adjust to present evils "over here".'

The new thing that Martin Luther King brought into protest was the conviction that the only Christian weapon is love. This principle he took to the limit. A bomb was exploded in the porch of his house. The crowd were out for trouble. 'We must love our white brothers', he said, 'no matter what they do to us. We must make them know that we love them. Jesus still cries out across the centuries, "Love your enemies". This is what we must live by. We must meet hate with love.' And a white policeman in the crowd was heard to say: 'If it hadn't been for that nigger preacher, we'd all be dead'.

In New York he was autographing copies of one of his books when a demented negro woman stabbed him. He was within a fraction of an inch off death. So near was the knife to piercing the aorta the surgeon said that if King had sneezed he would have died. He said of the woman who stabbed him: 'This person needs help. She is not responsible for the violence she has done me. Don't do anything to her; don't prosecute her, get her healed'.

When his followers were arrested during their marches or their boycotts, and when they were brought to court, they came wearing white crosses, with the words written on them: 'Father, forgive them; they know not what they do'.

This is a timely book for love is under challenge today.

Martin Luther King was not the first, nor will he be the last, to become a political protester armed only with the weapon of love. Even so, he was among the greatest of recent figures who have followed that path and his soul, like John Brown's, goes marching on. It was surprising to discover from this review of Kenneth Slack's book, that King's life was in danger several times

[1] Published by SCM PRESS, 1970.

before the final bullet which ended it performed its task. The American negro has achieved a great deal since King's time, recent as that was. Whether they have achieved enough is another matter, and one which will continue to haunt so long as good men—like Luther King— dream and toil.

ARTHUR SAMUEL PEAKE
J. T. Wilkinson

My time as a University student stretched from 1925 to 1933, and there was no one who did more for me and for my generation than A. S. Peake. We therefore welcome with open arms John T. Wilkinson's biography *Arthur Samuel Peake*.[1]

The most significant thing about Peake was that he remained a layman all his life. He was in fact the first English Nonconformist layman to be given a D.D. by a Scottish University—by Aberdeen in 1907. There never was a better equipped scholar in both Old and New Testament studies, but Peake never forgot the ordinary man. Criticism and interpretation do not end the duty of the teacher, so Peake held. 'He will steadily keep in view that his chief purpose is to deepen and expand the religious life of his readers.' When he was Dean of the Faculty of Theology in Manchester, he said of all University disciplines: 'The University sinks below the level of its privilege and duty unless it hears the call to share the gains of scholarship with those whose life runs in other grooves.' No man ever did more to bring scholarship to the ordinary man than Peake did.

He was a prodigious worker. Nearly all his books and articles were dictated. He had a phenomenal memory. He could lecture for an hour in perfect English and in lucid arrangement without a note of any kind. He used no manuscript in preaching, and seldom needed a hymn-book. He enjoyed the story of the American writer who wrote one article with his right hand, another with his left, dictated a third to his secretary, and in order to lose no time, rocked the cradle with his foot. He paid for his output, for by the time he was sixty he was an overtired man.

Peake's great contribution was that he brought to ordinary people a new view of the Bible, which liberated them from a narrow and rigid biblicism, and which yet did not offend and which left faith, not weaker, but stronger. 'He took hold of the 23rd Psalm', one of his students said of him, 'and taught us what it meant, and did more; he never left us till we had seen the shepherd.'

He was supremely efficient and could not tolerate inefficiency in others. He wrote to a contributor who was always late with his reviews: 'I only once heard Dr. Torrey preach, and he struck me as essentially a commercial traveller for God with a first-class line to offer! The best thing about his sermon was the text which showed a touch of genius in the collocation of two passages: "The Holy Ghost saith, Today; the fool saith, Tomorrow." I pass on the text as a word in season!'

On occasion he had a mordant wit. Once he continued to lecture after the bell had rung, and the students, as students will, shuffled their feet 'Gentlemen', said Peake mildly, 'I have yet a few pearls to cast before I finish.'

Peake was a kind man. Deissmann spoke of 'the kind eyes of Dr. Peake'. On one occasion he gave a poor beggar-man some work to do in his garden, and then he wrote a letter to his regular gardener to explain, lest the regular gardener be hurt.

This book is a very worthy tribute to a very great man.

Barclay might surely be speaking of himself when he writes, in this review, that 'Peake's great contribution was

[1] Published by EPWORTH PRESS, 1971.

that he brought to ordinary people a new view of the Bible'. Those who are indebted to Peake's famous commentary and they are to be numbered in their thousands, will surely echo these words, *as will also those who have been enriched by this great scholar's other works. Sadly, his* magnum opus, *a commentary on Isaiah, never saw the light of day.*

BORN TO REBEL
B. E. Mays

'This book is the story of the lifelong quest of a man who desired to be looked upon first as a human being and secondarily as a black man.' That is a sentence from the introduction to the autobiography of Benjamin E. Mays.[1]

Simply to look at Benjamin Mays' record of achievement is to look apparently at a career of dazzling success. M. A. and Ph.D. of Chicago, an honorary doctor of no fewer than twenty-eight institutions, including Harvard and Emory, a vice-president of the Federal Council of Churches of Christ in America, President of the Atlanta Board of Education, one of the four chosen representatives of the United States of America at the funeral of Pope John, for twenty-seven years the President of Morehouse College, and many another distinction—what more could a man want? And yet this is the book of a profoundly dissatisfied man, a man in whom the injustices meted out to the American negro rankle and torture—for Benjamin Mays is black.

Here is the first paragraph of the book: 'I remember a crowd of white men who rode up on horseback with rifles on their shoulders. I was with my father when they rode up, and I remember starting to cry. They cursed my father, drew their guns and made him salute, made him take off his hat and bow to them several times. Then they rode away. I was not yet five years old, but I have never forgotten them.'

Benjamin Mays had to fight for his education—even against his own father. He went to the State College in Orangeburg. One of his brothers gave him three dollars a month, and another three were necessary. He earned them at the stomach-turning job of cleaning out the latrines at night.

Benjamin Mays made it, but there are things that Benjamin Mays can neither forget nor disregard—and rightly. In 1921 in Atlanta a negro, working for a white woman, fell from a ladder and broke a leg. She called the ambulance, but made the mistake of calling it from a white station. The ambulance came and the driver left the negro lying in his pain and his blood until an ambulance from a black station should come. In 1966 Sam Oni an African student was refused entry to, and forcibly turned away from, Tattnall Square Baptist Church in Macon, Georgia.

It is true that the ministers of the church disagreed with this action, but they were ejected from their posts by the vote of the congregation.

Benjamin Mays, as we have said, is the holder of twenty-eight doctorates, yet in Atlanta which has been his home for thirty years only two white churches have ever invited him to speak to their congregation.

This is a disturbing book to read. Benjamin Mays writes: 'I have never sought "acceptance" as such, but I have wanted respect from all mankind. Love is wonderful; but if I could not have both, I would prefer respect'. This book is a great cry by a great man—and a great warning.

It is interesting to compare this review with the second piece in this book (see p. 5). This time he is considering a study of another great American negro; but this time an embittered one. What happened to Benjamin Mays, Honorary Doctor of Harvard and Vice-President to the Federal Council of Churches of

[1] Published by SCRIBNER & CO.

Christ in America, among many other distinctions, and particularly to his parents, is a story which Barclay clearly finds disturbing. The reference in this piece to the African student who was turned away from a Baptist Church in Georgia in 1966 may act as a reminder that a similar incident took place only recently during the Presidential campaign of Jimmy Carter. We may also reflect that for too many coloured folk in our own community feel they can best worship and serve God in their own (mushrooming) 'black churches' than in the already existing ones. . . .

PORTRAIT OF SOPER
William Purcell

It is not difficult to write the biography of a man while the man is still alive; it is impossible. And yet that is what William Purcell has tried to do.[1]

In his early youth Donald Soper, as Eric Baker said, was in danger of becoming the darling of the Connexion; he escaped that danger only to become its *enfant terrible.*

Donald Soper has always been afraid of nothing in the matter of saying things. He has a habit of speaking in headlines. He has rebuked the Queen for her interest in horse-racing and Prince Philip for playing polo on Sunday. He has wondered why, if we have the American more or less settled in this country, we should not have the Russians too. At the time of the Suez trouble he discerned a lot of good in Nasser, and in Devonport of all places he expressed the opinion that the armed forces should be done away with. A Socialist himself, he has wished that more members of the Labour Party were Socialists. Of the Church he has said: 'The Church is no longer a viable institution for the expression of Christianity and for the good of the world.' He has suggested that all reading of the Bible should be barred for a trial period of one year, and that every other sermon should be on a current political problem seen in the light of Christ. All his life he has been an uncompromising pacifist.

He is an honest man. F. R. Tennant was his tutor at Cambridge, and Tennant used to say that he would like to write outside his lecture-room: 'Eschew ambiguity, those who enter here'. Soper could never be accused of ambiguity. He was brought up in such a way that from his earliest days the Church was an essential and integral part of his life. But he did have a period, after reading Lecky's *History of Rationalism,* when he became an atheist. 'I have to live', he said, 'on the iron rations of a number of simple truths which I really do believe.'

He is a man with a concern for men and women. On entering the ministry, he was asked in the standard question, if he had a passion for souls. 'He was not aware, he confessed, of having a passion for souls. He was not quite sure what a soul was. But he had a great love for people.'

He can talk to ordinary men as few other clerics can. He will be for ever associated with his sessions on Tower Hill. He has been called the greatest open air preacher since Latimer preached at St. Paul's Cross. But on Tower Hill he does not so much preach as answer questions. He has said that the one ever-recurring problem is: 'Why does God send pain?' Beyond a doubt, there has been something apostolic about Tower Hill. At times he could be caught out. On one occasion a heckler was inveighing against the Eighteenth Amendment (Prohibition) in America. 'Have you been in America?' asked Soper. 'No', said the man. 'Then', said Soper, 'don't talk of things you know nothing of.' Instantly from the crowd there came the voice of a veteran atheist opponent: 'Have you ever been in Heaven?'

William Purcell has done the impossible task as well as it can be done. In this book a great twentieth century Christian, a modern gadfly like Socrates of old, comes vividly alive.

Published by A. R. MOWBRAY & CO., 1972.

It is unusual to find Barclay beginning a review with a flat statement of opinion. He does so here with the assertion that it is impossible to write the biography of a man who is still living. This leaves him in the position of having to comment on a book which, his judgment commits him to believe, was impossible to write. Even so, he still manages to be kind to it, stating that the writer has 'done the impossible task as well as it can be done'. And it is clear that he greatly admires the subject of the book, not only as a man of wit and courage but also as a passionate social Christian witness. It is appropriate that Barclay should respond so positively to this 'modern gadfly', for that rôle has been his own for many years, and we are all the better for it.

FRANCIS OF ASSISI
John Holland Smith

There are some men whose biography will never cease to be written so long as men write biographies at all; and there are some men whose tombs will be visited so long as the word saint has any meaning at all. And such a man is Francis of Assisi.

John Bernardone, for that was Francis' real name, was born in 1181 or 1182. He was the son of a well-to-do cloth merchant. Thomas of Celano says of him in the *'First Life'*: 'From his earliest years his parents brought him up without discipline, following the foolish standards of the world'. He had money and he 'did not hoard money avariciously, but squandered it open-handedly'. 'Until his twenty-fifth year he wasted his time woefully.' He was no scholar; he knew but little Latin. Somehow or other he learned French, talked French with his father's customers, wore French clothes, sang the French tunes of the troubadours and the jongleurs; and so they nicknamed him *il Francesco*, 'the Frenchman', and Francis he became.

So for twenty-five years he was the fashionable young man about town, the soldier, the troubadour, and then, as Celano says of him: 'God suddenly decided to deal with him'. Francis fell seriously ill, and the illness brought him to God. His sudden conversion separated him from his parents, got him treated as a madman, and chained him up as a prisoner, but Francis had begun on the path of no return.

It was then in the ruined chapel of St. Damian that out of the crucifix Francis heard the voice: 'Francis, rebuild my house; as you see, it is falling into total ruin'.

It was at the service of the Mass that he received his rule in the passage in which Jesus sends out his disciples to preach and heal, and to take absolutely nothing with them (Mt 10⁷⁻¹⁰). To that he was to add two other texts, the text which bade the rich young man, if he would be perfect, to sell all he had and to give to the poor (Mt 17²¹), and the text which bade the disciple take up his cross and follow Jesus (Mt 16²⁴). By these three texts Francis lived and would have all men live.

First, Francis was a man of utter poverty. His whole life was 'a challenge to Christian comfort'. In a Church which loved the power and the glory Francis was the little poor man.

Second, he preached forgiveness. 'Because our Lord Jesus Christ called a traitor "Friend",' he wrote, 'we must see as friends those from whom we have received pain and injustice, humiliation, torture, martyrdom and death.'

Third, he knew joy, not the strident joy of the horse-laugh, but the serene joy that no man takes from us. He was too happy for the orthodox.

Fourth, never was any man so much 'in Christ'. 'As he preached he did not look at his audience, but gazed up into the sky, as though expecting the supreme judge there to appear any second.'

This is an excellent biography,[1] and notably free from the sentimentality with which Francis is too often surrounded.

There appears to be a veritable industry of St. Francis biographies and several have appeared since this one, which was written in 1972. This may be

[1] Published by SIDGWICK & JACKSON, 1972.

because there is something dateless about the story of Francis, a story of gaiety and beauty, which appeals to all ages and generations. So Barclay contents himself here with a brief re-telling of the story itself, inter-spersing it with memorable comments of his own such as, 'he knew joy, not the strident joy of the horse-laugh, but the serene joy that no man takes from us'. Joy has been a constant feature of Barclay's work too.

C. S. LEWIS: A BIOGRAPHY
R. Lancelyn Green and Walter Hooper

When a man has distinguished himself in a great number of fields, there is much to be said for a biography of him which is straightforward and chronological, and which leaves the more elaborate treatment of the separate fields to those who are experts therein. Roger Lancelyn Green and Walter Hooper have given us just such a biography —and a most valuable book it is.[1]

Few people have had so wide an appeal to so many of the sections of the public as C. S. Lewis had.

He was to begin with a man of the highest academic distinction. A double first of Oxford, Honorary Fellow of University and of Magdalen College, Oxford, and of Magdalene College, Cambridge; Hon. D.D. of St. Andrews and Hon. D.Litt., of Manchester; Fellow of the British Academy and Fellow of the Royal Society of Literature, holder of the Gollancz Memorial Prize for Literature, and the Carnegie Medal for the best children's book of 1956, Professor of Mediaeval and Renaissance Literature at Cambridge— the academic world had honoured him, although to some academics he was suspect because he was a bestselling author.

He was a man whom the common people heard gladly. Once in a transport café he was the centre of animated conversation. One of the transport men asked a friend of Lewis's who Lewis was. He was told and was astonished. 'Blimey', he said, 'he's a toff, he is! A real nice bloke!'—a tribute which Lewis regarded as the greatest compliment he had ever been paid.

He was perhaps the only apologist for Christianity to whom the sophisticated sceptics would listen. Chad Walsh called him 'apostle to the Skeptics'; and Charles Moorman said of him that he was 'a cocktail party *Advocatus Christi*.

There was in Lewis an element of simplicity. He was simple in his pleasures. 'You can't', he said, 'get a cup of tea large enough or a book long enough to suit me.' He was simple in his worship and could not stand what he called 'liturgical fidget'. He was basically simple in his beliefs. 'The Christian rule', he said, 'is, "Either marriage, with complete faithfulness to your partner, or else total abstinence"'. Very early he said: 'I don't think anything, even an undergraduate clique, can live on denials'. There were for him greater things than the Christian apologetic in which he was so expert. 'A man', he said, 'can't always be defending the truth; there must be a time to feed on it.' 'The work of a Beethoven and the work of a charwoman', he insisted, 'become spiritual on precisely the same condition, that of being offered to God, on being done humbly "as to the Lord".'

Loyalty was part of the very nature of C. S. Lewis, and the way in which from 1917 to 1951, at the cost of his own comfort, he took upon himself responsibility for the wife and sister of his friend Paddy Moore, killed in battle, is an epic of what it means to be true to an obligation.

From this book C. S. Lewis emerges a living, vital figure, not least because in his life the authors were very close to him, and write not as duty but *con amore*.

Perhaps no one has yet come up with a truly in-depth study of C. S. Lewis 'the only apologist for Christianity', as

[1] Published by WM. COLLINS & SONS, 1974.

Barclay describes him, 'to whom the sophisticated sceptics would listen'. Certainly, at the time of the publication of this book in 1974, there were those among its reviewers who felt that it did not measure up to the stature of its subject. All the more interesting, therefore, to find Barclay taking a different view, his customary reluctance to condemn overcoming whatever hesitations he may possibly have felt. Or it may be that he found the book easy to like, noting among its virtues the fact that the joint-writers knew Lewis personally and wrote with a genuine love of him.

THE DOOR WHEREIN I WENT
Lord Hailsham

'One man in his time', said Shakespeare, 'plays many parts.' When these parts include the taking of a double first at Oxford, being President of the Oxford Union, being leader at one time or another of both the House of Commons and the House of Lords, twice being minister of Education, being the first minister of Science, being Lord Chancellor, being a Fellow of the Royal Society, the man who has played all these parts is bound to have in his life a story worth telling. Lord Hailsham has given us such a story.

This story is not in the normal sense of the term an autobiography.[1] It was Lord Hailsham's aim 'to betray no confidences, to injure no friends, to confess no intimate indiscretions, and to claim no particular credit for thinking and acting as I have done'. The book is no book of political gossip; it is the story of a spiritual odyssey from faith to faith.

Faith has never been an easy thing for Lord Hailsham. 'I am', he writes, 'one of those condemned to live this life in the discipline of darkness, and therefore in doubt, in faith but without certainty.' Nevertheless he has 'genuine and coherent and related views of life and its meaning which give me sense and direction in all I do, consolation in misfortune and courage when tempted to despair'.

He was by no means always like this. When he was seventeen years of age and at Eton, his mother died totally unexpectedly. In the afternoon the headmaster came to comfort him. 'He was a gentleman and a Christian. He sought to console me with talk about the afterlife. I was discourteous. I suddenly realized that I did not believe a word of what he was saying, and I told him so. Nevertheless for the sake of his father

and for the sake of others who loved him he made no open break with the Church.

He has the strongest possible belief in a kind of natural law of morality. He came on a letter written by his grandfather to a student who was losing his faith. 'For ever truth is better than falsehood, beauty than ugliness, justice than injustice, kindness than cruelty. These few truths, believe me, are worth more than half the creeds.' It means that somewhere there is something which gives validity to such value judgments; and may we not in the end talk not of some *thing*, but of 'him', and if of him then also 'thou'? Of prayer Hailsham says: 'It consists in a kind of feeling of spiritual sunbathing turning oneself to the spiritual light and allowing it to revive the spirit, like the sunlight on a flower, or a mother's smile on the child'.

'To me', writes Hailsham, 'law is the first of the social services.' Law must be 'rational, simple and practical'. The function of law is to make it be seen that force does not pay. *Agapē*, in Latin *caritas* (hence 'charity'), is 'the art of being a dear'.

Hailsham's political aim is 'privately-owned industry, and publicly-owned social service'. He says finely: 'No Christian may think of himself as a success if he contemplates seriously any of his shortcomings. Equally no Christian will think of himself as a failure if he reflects on the love of Christ for himself.'

This is a great book, for it shows a fine mind grappling with the problems of life and faith.

[1] Published by WM. COLLINS & SONS, 1975.

Better known in his earlier days as Quintin Hogg, Lord Hailsham, sometime Lord Chancellor of England, among many other distinctions, has been a public figure for many years. This book, published in 1975 is, as Barclay is careful to stress, not an auto-biography but a spiritual odyssey. Its fascination—and this obviously looms large with Barclay—lies in the fact that it represents something of the struggles of a first class mind to cope with religious doubt and to find its way to a living faith. It is clear that Barclay has no difficulty both in greatly admiring the book, and in being strongly attracted to its subject. His selection of quotations is, as usual, significant, such as: 'no Christian may think of himself as a success if he contemplates seriously any of his shortcomings. Equally no Christian will think of himself as a failure if he reflects on the love of Christ for himself'. We have sought to highlight some of the main motifs of Barclay's writings, both in the Introduction and in footnotes to his reviews. Here is another one, which is of telling importance in Barclay 'the popularizer'; namely his great sympathy with those enmeshed in doubt.

II The Affairs of Man

A SOUTH INDIA DIARY
J. E. Lesslie Newbigin

This was bound to be an interesting book because it is written by a Church of Scotland minister who became Bishop of Madhurai and Ramnad in the Church of South India.[1]

In the Foreword Bishop Newbigin gives a fascinating account of the steps by which union in South India was reached. The fourfold basis of that union is extremely interesting. It consists of four points. (a) The Holy Scriptures of the Old and New Testament as containing all things necessary to salvation, and as being the full and ultimate standard of faith. (b) The Apostles' Creed, as the baptismal symbol; and the Nicene Creed as the sufficient standard of the Christian Faith. (c) The two sacraments ordained by Christ Himself—Baptism and the Supper of the Lord—ministered with unfailing use of Christ's words of institution, and of the elements ordained by Him. (d) The Historic Episcopate, locally adapted in the methods of its administration to the vaying needs of the nations and peoples called of God into the Unity of the Church. Truly the United Church started from a magnificent beginning.

In Bishop Newbigin's diocese there are five hundred and fifty village congregations, two colleges, six high schools, three training schools, two industrial schools and about one hundred and sixty ordinary elementary schools. He is impressed with the danger of becoming immersed in administration. 'Ministration is swallowed up in administration.' 'There is a terrible danger that the Church should become a large social service organization with its centre in a modern streamlined office rather than God's family with its centre in the apostles' teaching, and fellowship, the breaking of bread and prayers.'

The spirit in which the Union was achieved and is carried out is truly Christian. At one meeting of the Synod some one said: 'The demand to know where we are going is one which no Christian has a right to make'. Bishop Newbigin says: 'At the last meeting [of his pastors and presbyters] I put a large Bible on the table and pointed out that our constitution was already there, and we were only making local rules'.

The great impression of this book is that here the history of the Early Church is being re-enacted.

There is not a page of this book without interest. As we follow Bishop Newbigin touring his diocese in ramshackle buses, in bullock carts, in his own car, on the pillion of a motor bicycle which could climb mountains, on foot, we get again the authentic thrill of the Acts of the Apostles. When one has finished his book one does not want to criticize it; one wants to get to one's knees and pray that the modern apostles of the Church of South India may be blessed and strengthened in their task.

The Church of South India, inaugurated in the September of 1947 by the union of four of the dioceses of the Anglican Church of India, Burma and Ceylon, the South India Province of the Methodist Church, and in the South India United Church, was hailed in its time as something of an epoch-making event on the long road towards Church unity. The book which Barclay reviews here consists of the recollections of one who, as a bishop in that newly constituted Church, saw something of its life at first hand.

[1] Published by SCM PRESS, 1960.

NAUGHT FOR YOUR COMFORT
Trevor Huddleston

On 12th January, 1837, Carlyle's 'History of the French Revolution' was first published. Naturally Carlyle's friends wondered what the critics and reviewers would do with it. Carlyle's answer was: 'You have not had for a hundred years any book that came more direct and flamingly from the heart of a living man. Do what you like with it, you——' If one thing is certain about Father Trevor Huddleston's book, it is that it is written directly and flamingly from the heart.

Father Huddlestone is a member of the Anglican Community of the Resurrection. He did not go to Africa with a burning zeal to be a social reformer; the conditions of South Africa set alight that flame within him. He makes no attempt to write this book with judicial detachment. 'What I shall try to avoid is that most common and persistent error in all such assessments—the attempt to be impartial. By this I mean that I shall write this book as a partisan, for I believe that Christians are committed in the field of human relationships to a partisan approach. I believe that, because God became Man, therefore human nature in itself has a dignity and value which is infinite. I believe that this conception naturally carries with it the idea that the State exists for the individual, not the individual for the State. Any doctrine based on racial or colour prejudice and enforced by the State is therefore an affront to human dignity and "ipso facto" an insult to God Himself.'

Father Huddleston believes that in South Africa there is no such thing as justice for the coloured people. The African convict-labourer, Elias Mpikwa, was beaten to death with a hope-pipe by the farmer for whom he was working. The farmer was found guilty of nothing worse than common assault. Not even the equity of the law can protect the coloured people as Father Huddleston sees it.

Father Huddleston believes that there is in South Africa no hope of true education for the coloured people. In August, 1954, the South African Government made it quite impossible for the Mission Schools to continue. The Bantu Education Act declares that the aim of education is to equip the Bantu child 'for his future work and surroundings'. But in introducing the Bill Dr. Verwoerd said: 'I want to remind Hon. Members that if the native of South Africa today, in any kind of schools in existence, is being taught to expect that he will live his adult life under a policy of equal rights, he is making a big mistake'. It is 'education for servitude'.

Even in the Church the coloured people have no real rights. The Rev. C. B. Brink of the Dutch Reformed Church said: 'It is true that the unity of the congregation of Christ is clearly shown at the Table of the Lord. At the moment, however, a common Communion of all races on a large scale in South Africa would scarcely be edifying'.

Father Huddleston has no doubt that the Christian is bound to use every effort to fight this racialism.

As we read this book, we will be moved to exclaim: 'Thank God that the prophets are not yet dead'.

Barclay is reviewing here the 1971 edition of a book which first appeared in 1956. Described as 'the book which stirred the conscience of the world' it

[1] Published by WM. COLLINS & SONS, 1971.

was that rare event: a work of genuine prophecy. Father Huddleston, as he then was, the Bishop of Stepney as he is now, pointed to the inevitability of events in South Africa which have now taken place, and which will almost certainly lead to an even graver situation, as the recent riots in Soweto have shown.

Huddleston is now officially excluded from the country he writes about. 'Thank God', says Barclay, 'that the prophets are not yet dead.' This book, with its strong emphasis on the belief that any racial or colour prejudice is an insult to God himself, makes plain that they are not.

MAN'S ESTIMATE OF MAN
E. H. Robertson

Pope was right when he said:
The proper study of mankind is man.

Mr. E. H. Robertson has written a fascinating book[1] which is a book about man, and therefore a book about each person who will read it.

Man begins as a paradox.

Man is 'a sinner made in the image of God'. For that very reason his sin is all the more serious, 'for the sin of a good man is more serious than that of an evil man'. And also for that very reason 'man's true greatness lies not in what he is, but in what he is becoming'. But man has to face a paradox, not only in his personal relationships with himself, but also in his relationship to the world. He is part of the world, and therefore he is on the way to death. But at the same time he is apart from the world, and can stand back and look at the world and death and himself.

He will be offered various ways out of his dilemma. The Freudian will tell him that the *ego* is under three pressures. There is the *id*, which consists of the powerful, primitive urges of the unconscious, implanted there by personal and racial experience—and always directed towards the pleasure principle, of which the most powerful force is sex. There is the pressure of the laws and rules of the society in which he lives. And there is 'the arch-villain of the piece', the *super-ego*, which is what the Christian would call conscience, and which erects prohibitions against the free expression of the *id*. The Freudian solution is to destroy the *super-ego*, and therefore to destroy the validity of ethical standard altogether.

There is the way of the existentialist. For him 'man is not classified, he is observed'. In life there is a weariness, a fog, an abyss of existence, an utter indifference. There are no standards; life is to be accepted as reality as it is in the individual experience.

There are in the life of man three fears, which need three courages to meet them, as Tillich has pointed out. There is *the fear of fate and death*. There is *the fear of emptiness and loss of meaning*. There is *the fear of guilt and condemnation*.

Man is faced with three ways. He can seek to lose himself in God. There is the way of encounter in which a man tries to discover God. Finally, there is the way of simple acceptance. A man has to accept the amazing fact that 'forgiveness without reason matched sin without excuse'. In the end all a man can do is take.

Mr. Robertson has brought to the writing of this book wide theological knowledge, penetrating insight into human nature, and a glowing devotion—a rare combination which results in a rare book.

The writer of this book, a Baptist minister, who was also for a period Assistant Head of Religious Broadcasting at the B.B.C., has always been a man with an enquiring mind. To review a book of this order in so short a space, must obviously have been a difficult undertaking, but Barclay acts here as an interpreter clarifying and compressing a difficult argument into a more readable form. This is, as he says, 'a rare book'. It is also a clear instance of the Barclay of whom it may truly be said that 'Everyman, I will go with thee, and be thy guide; in thy most need to go by thy side'.

Published by SCM PRESS, 1958.

A CHRISTIAN OF EAST GERMANY
J. Hamel

When Bengel the great commentator was commenting on Paul's phrase 'the Church of God which is at Corinth', he did so in one of his epigrammatic sentences—'the Church of God which is at Corinth contains within itself an immense and joyous paradox'. It is precisely that same paradox which is contained in the title of this deeply moving and a thrilling book.[1] The book is translated by Ruth and Charles West and has an Introduction by Charles C. West.

Johannes Hamel is a pastor in East Germany; he does not play down the discomforts, the difficulties, the dangers of that task, but in spite of it all there is a certain radiance in this book: 'It is a great thing to live in the East Zone'. 'A pastor in the West must long to come over to us, much as in the old days a young knight often longed for the day of his testing!'

The bitterness of trying to be a Christian in a Communist state is that so often there comes the temptation to live a lie. But the extraordinary thing is what happens again and again when the Christian witness is made.

A girl student during an illness was visited by other Christian students and became a Christian. She was then visited by a Communist official who told her bluntly that she would not be admitted to a certain examination unless she joined the Communist Party. In conscious falsehood she joined the Party. She came in great distress to her pastor; she felt that she could no longer remain within the Christian fellowship, not because she did not want to be a Christian but because her whole life was a lie. She was persuaded to attend both Party and Church, and she was torn in two. Then one day, unable to stand the tension any longer, not caring what happened, she handed in her resignation to the Party, and peace descended on her. The Party officials warned her that she was flinging away everything. She fearlessly chose to go on. The Party officials, note, the Communists, said to her: 'What you did, so shortly before the examination time, was unbelievably courageous. We need people like you. The riff-raff and the opportunists we will shake off one day in any case'. And in the end the Communists admitted the girl to the examination and to a job because they could not do without people with character like that.

We read of the Communist University Professor in search of assistants. 'Please send me Christians', he said, 'they are the only ones I can rely on.'

The Student Christian Fellowship was being far too successful for the peace of mind of the Communist Officials. They planned to infiltrate their own agents into it, to destroy the Fellowship from the inside. The plan failed. 'Those we send on this errand', said the bewildered Party officials, 'come back Christians!'

This is a tremendous book; and it is the blazing proof that the defence against Communism lies in the Christian life and the Christian faith. The only real defence of Christianity is the Christian. This is the lesson which this book teaches. God grant that we may learn it!

This book speaks of the experiences of a Christian in East Germany. The review is a sombre reminder of how little has changed on the religious scene on the other side of the Iron Curtain. The

[1] Published by SCM PRESS, 1960.

persecutions, and penalties attached to the profession of the Christian faith, still apply and it can still be a considerable material handicap to a young person's future career to be known as a practising Christian. Since this review came out there has been much discussion about détente between the West and the Soviet block, but whether détente has yet impinged upon the Christian scene is doubtful. Meanwhile, as Barclay says, in situations of stress and persecution 'the only real defence of Christianity is the Christian'. For him, the only real test of Christian belief is Christian conduct.

COME OUT THE WILDERNESS
Bruce Kenrick

Sometimes we wonder if there is still such a thing as the power of the Gospel and sometimes we get unmistakable and indisputable evidence that there is. We are presented with such evidence in this book,[1] for this is the story of how the Church came to East Harlem in the person of some young men.

In that area more than 200,000 people live jammed together in little over one square mile. In one block 4000 people are packed into 27 rotting tenements. In one tenement 27 persons, including seventeen children and an eight-day-old infant, were housed in four basement coal-houses. each grimy cubicle being rented for 40 dollars a month. The tenements are rat- and cockroach-infested; the garbage is left to accumulate and to rot; landlords will do nothing to make premises habitable, and, if any complaint is made, a man will find himself on the street, without even a slum to live in.

Away back in 1947 a group of students and young ministers moved in to try to answer the question: 'Is the Gospel big enough for this?' That group was to become not only an experiment in evangelism but also an achievement in ecumenicity, for it contained Baptists, Brethren, Congregationalists, Episcopalians, Reformed, Methodists, Mennonites, and Presbyterians; and it had the support of no fewer than eight major denominations.

One of the main problems was the police. They were savage, brutal, racketeering and unjust. 'What we need', said a local chemist, 'is not protection by the police, but protection *from* the police.'

One of the greatest handicaps was the Church's actual history of other-worldliness and detachment from the life situation. 'Most of East Harlem's residents held that if God wasn't interested in their world, in their plumbing, in their Welfare allowance, in their need for good police, if God wasn't interested in such earthly issues, then they just weren't interested in God—He was irrelevant.'

If it was claimed: 'Politics is a dirty game; we Christians must keep out of it', the answer was: 'Politics is certainly a dirty game; we Christians must get into it and help to do away with the dirt'.

One of the terrible and tragic evils in Harlem was drug-taking. Of sixteen lads in a youth group, ten years later seven were addicts and one was dead through using drugs.

To this terrible situation the group brought only one weapon—love and caring. They had to love and they had to stick around, because Jesus loves and sticks around—and the worse a man is the more he needs that love.

No mass conversions are being claimed, but nonetheless a miracle happened. In East Harlem a little bit of the body of Christ became visible and alive in the church which was born there, 'a visible body of Christians who have risen as it were from their East Harlem grave'.

This is a deeply moving book, which it would be well for everyone in the Church to read, for here in Harlem the grace of Christ is still shining like a light in a dark place.

'The Wilderness' is in this case East Harlem. The story is that of a variegated group of Christians who moved there in 1947 in order to try and live out the question as to whether

[1] Published by WM. COLLINS & SONS, 1965.

the Gospel was big enough to be effective and relevant in so heart-breaking and challenging a situation of social degradation. Barclay claims this as 'a deeply moving book which it would be well for everyone in the Church to read'. It should not be overlooked that this review is not from a scholar snugly ensconced in his ivory tower, but one who has worked for many years in a city with notorious slums; who worked there in a deeply involved way, and who eventually became Honorary President of the YMCA, Glasgow.

THE SEEDS OF PEACE
Dewi Morgan

It is always true that one half of the world does not know how the other half lives, and it is particularly true that the inhabitants of a comfortable welfare state have little conception of what life can be like for the less fortunate parts of the world. One of the romances of modern Christendom is The Division of Inter-Church Aid. Refugee and World Service, which is a child of the World Council of Churches. In general we may call this work Christian Aid. Dewi Morgan tells something of the work in Algeria, Iran, Korea and India—and a thrilling and a moving story it is.[1]

When Algeria gained its independence it was devastated. It is a land where of the Moslem population 87.6 per cent, of the male and 96.9 per cent of the female population cannot read. Young men are allowed by the government to choose between compulsory military service and enrolment in the literacy corps. It is a land where in the urban areas the infant mortality is 90–110 per thousand and in the rural areas 150–160 per thousand. The need was clamant.

It was met in part by one of the most imaginative schemes of relief ever conceived. Soil erosion is the problem of Algeria. That problem was exacerbated by the savage action of the French in napalm-bombing the forest areas where there were trees. So a certain M. Jean Carbonare had the idea: 'Why don't we devise a scheme to help the unemployed plant trees?' Men would be given work; soil erosion would be halted; and the future would be cared for. The scheme began. Today there are twenty large seedling nurseries and a hundred and more baby forests.

This work has meant the use of lorries and tractors and sawmills and this has given the chance for six-month courses for apprentices. Life is being changed. And mark this —this is not work done by Christians for Christians; it is work done by Christians for human beings, for in the city of Constantine for example there are 250,000 inhabitants and not as many as 200 Christians.

In Iran, in the area of which Esmatabad is a village, at 10.52 p.m. on 1st September 1962 an earthquake struck and in a sixty by twenty-five mile area in moments 11,300 were killed and 20,000 rendered homeless. Christian Aid was called in; Esmatabad was its area. In two years 306 new houses were built, a well was sunk, schools were erected, the face of the place was changed. And mark this—in Iran, apart from 50,000 Armenian Christians and 20,000 Nestorians, there are only about 2500 Christians in a population of 20,000,000. Once again it is help to brother-men in the name of Christ.

Here is Christianity in action. Often the Christians working together do not know to which denomination the other belongs and all they see in the sufferer is a human being who needs the love of Christ. Here is a book which moves and which challenges us to ask ourselves, What are we doing to help?

Since this review was written many disasters, both natural and man-made, have brought forth help from Christian Aid. From earthquake to revolution, from drought to flood-disaster, the procession seems endless. As Barclay so rightly comments, Christian Aid is Christianity in action. The question which Barclay raises, however, remains: 'what are we doing to help?'.

[1] Published by HODDER & STOUGHTON.

SHAW IN HIS TIME
I. Brown

It is given to few men to become a legend in their own life-time, but it certainly was so with George Bernard Shaw. It is now fifteen years since Shaw died, and Ivor Brown has written a fascinating volume which is not so much a biography of Shaw as the setting of Shaw and his work in the context of his time.[1]

Shaw had not on the face of it a very thrilling start in life. The Shaws in Dublin, he himself said, were 'Somebodies on the way to becoming Nobodies'. He began his working life as a junior clerk in an estate agency, filing letters and taking impressions of them in a copying press and all for a salary of eighteen pounds a year. He was not in the technical sense very well educated and he never went to what would be called a good school.

From the beginning he was a Puritan in essence. Even in matters of food and drink he was a vegetarian and a total abstainer. 'I flatly declare', he said, 'that a man fed on whisky and dead bodies cannot do the finest work of which he is capable'. There were two Shaws—the prophet 'with the doctrine in his head', and 'the jester with a joke on his lips'.

For the original Puritans the theatre had been the means of *corruption*; for Shaw it was the means of *correction*. If he could teach his favourite theories 'with the warmth of the players' stage instead of with the austerity of a lecturer's dais', then he might get somewhere. 'He did not seek money; he sought believers.'

Sometimes Shaw went in for shock tactics. He made his famous verdict on Shakespeare: 'With the single exception of Homer, there is no eminent writer, not even Sir Walter Scott, whom I can despise so entirely as I despise Shakespeare'.

But in that very same notice he went on immediately to say that he pitied the man who did not enjoy Shakespeare and to pay massive tribute to the human qualities of the man. 'He has outlasted thousands of abler thinkers and will outlast thousands more.' It was idolatry that Shaw objected to.

Whatever Shaw might sometimes seem to be, he was a man with a purpose. 'To plod and keep the passion fresh' was his aim. 'I no longer desire happiness,' he said, 'life is nobler than that.' To be part of a purpose, and to work for it until exhausted was for him life.

However critical he might be of orthodox religion, he was still more critical of atheism. 'I am religious enough,' he said, 'to have spent a great part of my life trying to clean up the heavily barnacled creeds and make them credible, believing, as I do, that Society cannot be held together without religion.'

Mr. Brown in view of all the paradoxes which were Shaw says: 'If Dickens could be called a mob as well as a man, Shaw can similarly be described as the mixture of a brains trust and a mass meeting'.

This is an excellent book, written with erudition, with sympathy, and charm. It will pay the preacher to read of the playwright who was also a prophet.

It is a long time since the death of Shaw and Ivor Brown, the author of this book, so it is all the more interesting to note here those features which have continued to be noticeable in Barclay's reviews: tolerance, the ability

[1] Published by NELSON & CO., 1965.

to extract interesting details tendency to be kind to the writers reviewed. *This review demonstrates all three characteristics. Shaw's great aim, as* cited above, was 'to plod and keep the passion fresh'. A well chosen epithet by one whose immense literary activity continues unabated!

CHILDREN IN NEED
A. Denney

There is no one for whom Christianity has done more than the child. Even in our own day child education and child welfare have taken great strides forward, particularly in the way in which child care and guidance are not now directed to punishment but rather 'to prevent and forestall' the possibility of harm to the child and damage by the child. Anthony Denney, the Research Officer of the Church of England Children's Council, has written an excellent account of what is being done and what needs to be done.[1]

Education is no longer the mere imparting of facts or even of skills. 'Education is the imparting to them (the children) of experience accompanied by interpretation and insight so given that the child is constantly acquiring the ability to make his own interpretations and gain his own insights. He must be loved and forgiven before he can love and forgive, he must receive mercy before he can himself be merciful, he must see Christ in others before he knows what he can possess Him for himself.' This involves teaching by being. If this is true of teachers, it is still truer of parents, and Mr. Denney in a magnificent phrase speaks of 'the ministerial function of parenthood'.

There are certain basic things which all children need. They need *acceptance* by adults other than in the family circle. They need *security*, so that they can feel safe. They need *the recognition of personal achievement*. It is in fact true that, when a child does badly, it may well be, not the fault of the child's ability, but of the parents' apathy. They need *the opportunity of extending experience* by moving out to new people and new spheres.

The worst deprivation that a child can suffer is not in material things, but rather the lack in his life of 'emotional warmth'.

There is here certain practical advice for those who would seek to help work with deprived children, or indeed with any children. The first essential is *reliability*. There must be 'a continued relationship on which the child can come to depend'. The erratic worker may be doing more harm than good. The second essential is that the worker must be in the work for the sake of the work. Dr. Kellmer Pringle points out that, 'if gratitude is expected for what is offered, it would be wiser not to attempt this particular kind of social service'. The person who must be thanked is a problem in other places than work among children!

There is a very fine definition of marriage and of what a home should be; there is a very fine section on the importance of play, there is an excellent section on the problem of working mothers and another on delinquency.

Mr. Denney has excellent statistical tables and valuable lists of societies engaged in this work and a full bibliography.

This is a first-rate book written out of a rare compound of technical knowledge, practical experience, and Christian love.

What is being done and what still needs to be done for children—which is the theme of this book under review—is, of course, a problem without end. Inevitably, such a book soon dates, and this piece which notes such things as the need by children for acceptance, security, recognition of achievement, and

[1] Published by SCM PRESS, 1966.

opportunity of extending experience, now appears to some extent to be covering old ground. But that is no reason to denigrate it, or to undervalue the fairness of Barclay's review of a subject which should at all times be a matter of concern for people, whether Christian or not.

THE HEALING OF PERSONS
P. Tournier

There are few men who have done more to relate medicine and religion than Paul Tournier has done. It was as far back as 1940 that Dr. Tournier wrote this his first book and into it he put more of himself than into any of his books; it has now come to us in an English edition.[1]

For Paul Tournier medicine is the 'medicine of the person'. It is not the disease which has to be treated, but the patient, and the patient is necessarily a unity. 'Moral health, spiritual health, and physical health form one indivisible whole'.

If the doctor accepts this idea of medicine, then medicine becomes a most comprehensive thing. 'Man does not die', a doctor has said. 'He kills himself.' Paul Tournier is therefore quite sure that the doctor must use every technical resource at his disposal. But his task is half done, if he does not 'help the patient to solve the problems in his life'. The doctor may cure a man physically, but if he does nothing to show the man how to overcome the problems which the man has still to meet 'he is like a mother who abandons the child she has just brought into the world, leaving him helpless to face life'.

We may put this even more directly and simply and fundamentally. 'The highest role of the doctor', Tournier writes, 'is to help men to discern what is God's purpose for their lives and to conform therewith'. 'That is why I feel', he writes, 'that the deepest meaning of medicine is not in 'counselling lives', but in leading the sick to personal encounter with Jesus Christ.'

It is unnecessary to point out how revolutionary this is, and how it is impossible in the conveyor-belt methods of doctors' surgeries and hospital consultations in an over-crowded health service.

There are certain chapters of this book which are highly illuminating. Dr. Tournier has a very penetrating chapter on Flight, the means of escape which men seek. There is the *flight into dreams*, the *flight into the past*, the *flight into the future*, the *flight into disease*, the *flight into passivity*, the *flight into work*. And—worst of all—there is the *flight into religion*.

Again, Dr. Tournier has a penetrating analysis of attitudes to life. 'There are three roads in front of every man: reality without God, which is the dissociation of the materialists; God without reality, which is the dissociation of the pseudo-mystics; and, lastly, God with reality, which is the Christian faith.'

He tells of a highly intellectual man who would argue for hours about Christianity and who would yet never take the decisive step of becoming a Christian. 'One day he came back to see me and told me he had found Christ. He had met a Christian who had simply told him that he was an intellectual glutton.'

This is a great and a moving book, continually lit up by actual case-histories illustrating Dr. Tournier's methods and beliefs. Would that every doctor and every minister and parson would read this book! And would that all laymen would read it too!

Here, in contrast to the previous book is a subject which, although written in 1940, has not dated at all. As Barclay says, Doctor Tournier's book is a great and moving one, shot through with illuminating glimpses of truth which Barclay, as the good reviewer should, unerringly pinpoints.

[1] Published by WM. COLLINS & SONS, 1966.

Barclay warms to his theme here particularly because of the pastoral concern which energizes all his workings.

RACE: A CHRISTIAN SYMPOSIUM
C. S. Hill and D. Mathews (Eds.)

It might well be true to say that the supreme problem of the twentieth century is the race and colour problem. This is a magnificent contribution, if not to the solution, at least to the understanding of that problem.[1] The subjects dealt with in it are Migration in a World Setting, The Rights of Individuals and the Duties of States, Racial Images and Attitudes in Britain—the Background, The Psychology of Prejudice, The Biology of Race, The Christian View of Intermarriage, The Biblical Doctrine of Race, The Theology of Race, The Rôle of Christians; and also an Indian, a West Indian and an African immigrant give briefly their experiences in Britain.

David Mathews in the Introduction declares that 'tolerance is not enough'. It has to be realized that 'Britain, in practice and certainly in potential, has as much racial prejudice and discrimination as any other country'. And 'no one really believes that Christians are less prejudiced or less ignorant than anyone else'. The Indian immigrant finds Christians guilty of racial discrimination as anyone else. The African is compelled to question the sincerity of the missionary movement.

Sheila Patterson records that in 1953 a Dutch Reformed Church conference distinguished three attitudes: 'those who sincerely believe in a righteous racial separation in the Church based on the Scriptures; those who make no such confession but who nevertheless practise some form of separation because circumstances demand it; and those who are convinced that separation in the Church is wrong and stands condemned according to Scripture'. A fourth is also added by the same writer. 'Seventy years ago Ben Tillett told newly-arrived Jewish immigrant workers: "Yes, you are our brothers and we will do our duty by you. But we wish you had not come to this country".' And it could be that that last is the commonest of all.

The late Joost de Blank points out that the first two important questions put into the mouth of Almighty God are: 'Man, where are you?' and, secondly, 'Where is your brother?' But he goes on to quote the cynical saying of Lord Samuel: 'We are all brothers now, all Cains and Abels!'

One of the most interesting and significant things in the book is that again and again, on medical and on biological and on psychological grounds, the lie is given to the view that a mixture of races is bad, and that it produces an inferior creature.

By far the finest chapter in the book is that on The Psychology of Prejudice by Dr. David Stafford-Clark. It is a magnificent analysis. His solution is simple but radical. The basic human sin is self-centredness, the putting oneself in the centre of the picture instead of God.

When the expert in Psychological Medicine starts to preach, it is time we started to listen. This is an important book which will both instruct and shock.

The book he has before him reflects a fairly early stage in the great race relations debate. Whether it still both instructs and shocks, as Barclay claims it does, is open to question. Even so, it is interesting to note, how strongly Barclay applauds the view that tolerance is not enough, and emphasizes the fact that racial prejudice is frequently practised by the very people who in theory condemn it.

[1] Published by VICTOR GOLLANCZ, 1968.

RELIGION IN COMMUNIST CHINA
R. C. Bush Jr.

There is a terrible story of persecution in the modern Church, whether it be the persecution of violent death or of slow strangulation, told in this book.[1]

It is laid down in the Constitution of the People's Republic of China that: 'Citizens of China enjoy freedom of religious belief'. Strictly speaking and literally speaking, that may be true. But it does not include freedom of practice, activity or propagation. The belief is entirely internal; it must not affect conduct, relationship with other people or with the state. It gives no right whatever to meet, to worship, to preach or to perform religious acts of any kind.

On Marxist principles this should have happened by evolution. On these principles, religion, prayer, fear of the gods come from the fear of the forces of nature. This fear is used and fomented by the wealthy classes to keep the lower and the ignorant classes in spineless subjection. Learn the secrets of nature; then fear ceases. Introduce a classless society; then religion dies.

In China the greatest sin of Christianity and of the missionary movement was simply that it was foreign. 'All missionaries are spies' is the belief. Missionaries were no more than agents of western and capitalist propaganda. There is a grain of truth in this, for missionaries did come into China on the coat-tails of western political power. They did profit from unequal treaties and from various humiliations. They did adopt an attitude of paternalism; they did have a conscious racial superiority in some cases. There was too little attempt to build up an indigenous church. In Roman Catholic missions four out of every five bishops and two out of every three priests were not Chinese. And, amazingly,

the missionaries did not foresee the revolution at all. We cannot justify; but to some extent we can understand.

The government used every method to kill the Church. It used slander. Missionaries were charged with preaching that Christ 'was the liberator of mankind who advocated peace and opposed bloodshed and war', whereas this rôle belonged to Mao and the Communist party.

There was bitter persecution. 'Boiling hot tea was poured on the head of an evangelist's wife while she, her husband, and the minister were made to kneel all night next to a fire fed by bibles, hymnbooks and religious materials.'

The Chinese did introduce a church founded on the three autonomies—self-government, self-finance and self-propagation. But it was no more than a tool of the government with every Christian symbol removed and Communist symbols substituted. At least outwardly, the Chinese Church was killed. This book also tells the story of Islam, Buddhism, Confucianism and Taoism in Communist China. It is meticulously documented and written without any hysterics at all. It is a book which every Christian should read—on his knees.

China, which has in its time concealed so many secrets, keeps this one still. What has happened to religion in China and to Christianity in particular since the death of Chairman Mao remains a mystery. But, as Barclay points out, the story of Christian mission in China needs to be read by Christians today with repentance. It was a fundamental error

[1] Published by ABINGDON PRESS.

not to see the weakness of persisting with a Westernized form of Christianity. The consequence, inevitably, was that the *missionary was seen as a foreigner rather than a friend. And for that a high price has been paid.*

I KNOW IT WAS THE PLACE'S FAULT
Des Wilson

Every now and then there arises some person or some association of persons with the ability to catch the imagination and rouse the conscience of the public. This happened in this country with the birth of Shelter in 1966. Shelter insisted that both the public and the government should face the crude and brutal facts of the situation and condition in which some people have to live. And now Des Wilson has written a book calculated to stimulate the social conscience of this country even more.[1]

First, let us look at the statistical facts. In this country 'there are some three million families still living either in slums, near slums, or in grossly overcrowded conditions'. In Glasgow there are 100,000 houses unfit for habitation, 70,000 households without hot water and 180,000 people overcrowded. In London there are 100,000 unfit houses. In Liverpool there are 70,000 unfit houses and 40,000 households without hot water. In Birmingham there are 40,000 houses unfit for habitation, and 60,000 houses without hot water. The number of families on the Council waiting list is in Glasgow 50,000, in Birmingham 30,000, in London, 100,000.

Take the results of this. In such overcrowded buildings accidents are ten times more common than where the housing is good. In Newcastle as compared with the least overcrowded, in the most overcrowded there were twice as many cases of T.B.; venereal disease and offences against the person were five times more prevalent, and the figure for larceny was only a little less. Persons on probation were seven times more numerous; juvenile delinquents three times more numerous; cases of child neglect five or six times greater; mentally abnormal persons three times more numerous. A slum is an expensive item for a country to afford.

Take the facts as to among whom this poverty and bad housing are most common. 'What is even more unacceptable is that the largest single groups among the poor or borderline poor are poor because they work for the remainder. They are in the public services. They work on buses and trains, they deliver the post and collect the dustbins, they sweep the streets and clean and repair the drains, they work in hospitals, and schools and serve a society that is too selfish to serve them.'

This is a tragic story. Often people are making a brave fight for respectability in conditions like that; but suppose some of them are shiftless and feckless, Des Wilson says truly: 'The test of a compassionate society is the response it shows to the *undeserving* poor'.

If you do not want to be disturbed, don't read this book. The society which allows such conditions —especially a so-called affluent society—has no right to the name Christian.

The story of Des Wilson and Shelter, an organization which came into being to face the challenge of the housing crisis among the underprivileged in Britain, is well known. What has made it well known is more the frequency with which the media give prominence to the problem, than to documentation of the true facts. But here many of the facts can be found in book form, and Barclay clearly finds the result most disturbing, as well he

[1] Published by OLIPHANTS, 1970.

may. As he said at the time of this review 'if you do not want to be disturbed don't read this book'. It might also be said that 'If you don't want to be disturbed, don't think about Shelter'.

SOCIALISM IN BRITAIN FROM THE INDUSTRIAL REVOLUTION TO THE PRESENT DAY

T. L. Jarman

It is impossible to understand what any institution is, unless we first understand how it came to be what it is. That is why this is so interesting and important a book.

The word *socialist* was first used in an Owenite publication in 1827. The question is put 'whether it is more beneficial that capital should be individual or common', and it is then said that those who believe that it should be common are 'the communists and socialists'. To the end of the day this remains the basis of socialism. Keir Hardie, who, it is said, got more of his socialism from Robert Burns than from Karl Marx, declared that: 'Socialism means fraternity founded on justice, and the fact that in order to secure this it is necessary to transfer land and capital from private to public ownership is a mere incident in the campaign'. This is the essence of the famous Clause 4 which states the aim of the socialist party: 'To secure for the workers by hand or by brain the full fruits of their industry and the most equitable distribution thereof that may be possible, upon the basis of the common ownership of the means of production'. At the party conference of 1929 the words 'distribution and exchange' were added.

The process can be 'evolutionary or revolutionary'. In Britain it is always the evolutionary emphasis which had been dominant, and the means has often been taken to be education. As William Lovett, the Chartist leader said: 'How can a corrupt government stand against an enlightened people?'

The necessity for socialism came from two things. It came from the vast increase in production, made possible by the mechanization of the Industrial Revolution. And it came from the dramatic increase in population. The population of England and Wales was six millions in 1750, nine millions in 1801, eighteen millions in 1851.

All this produced a human and social situation which George Bernard Shaw illustrated in terms of land. First, people come and take for themselves common land, and the first-comers take the best. Bit by bit all the land is taken. Those with the best can in the end sit back and let theirs out and do nothing but live on the proceeds. But all the time there is building up a body of people for whom there is no land left, and who, even if there was any land, would have no money to buy it, and all they have to sell is themselves. So the serf, the labouring man is born.

In its early days socialism was tied up with the Christian Church.

The early socialists saw their socialism as a means of putting their Christianity into practical effect. It is one of the supreme tragedies—and indeed failures—of the Church, that the Church lost these and such as these.

Among many other good things this book has excellent sections on Robert Owen and Karl Marx. It would be difficult to find a book of greater sheer interest than this.

Things move fast in politics. Britain, where a socialist government has long ceased to be a surprise but more a fact of life, has seen such changes that it may seem surprising to come across a book which examines Socialism as a phenomenon. In reviewing it, Barclay for once gives the impression

[1] Published by VICTOR GOLLANCZ, 1972.

of being on rather unfamiliar ground. Perhaps that is why he uncritically reproduces Bernard Shaw's over-simplification of the social situation in which he alleges Socialism had its origin. But Barclay is certainly right in pointing to the early association between Socialism and the Christian church, although whether he is equally correct in representing this as yet another lost opportunity is open to question.

THE PURITAN PLEASURE OF THE DETECTIVE STORY
Erik Routley

I have only one complaint about detective stories—there aren't enough of them. That is why I approached Dr. Erik Routley's book with the keenest anticipation—and I was not disappointed.[1]

Dr. Routley's book begins with a mystery. He begins by telling a story about Henry Wheeler Robinson, Doctor of Divinity, Principal of an Oxford College, one of the greatest Old Testament scholars of his day. Wheeler Robinson, so it is said, in Oxford railway station went to the book-stall. He looked at the selection of detective stories and found he had read them all. He asked the attendant if any more were in stock, and was directed to another part of the stall. 'Read 'em all', he said again. On request the attendant produced another supply from under the counter. 'Read 'em all', came Wheeler-Robinson's comment again, whereat the attendant leaned across the counter and said, 'Well, sir, all I can suggest is that perhaps you might try some serious literature for a change'. A good story! But, with the one difference that the scene is Blackwell's and not the railway station, exactly the same story is told of A. S. Peake. The biblical pundits would say that here we have a floating legend, and many a man has written a thesis on less!

Dr. Routley has an examination of the reasons why people read detective stories. Some read for the intellectual satisfaction that the solution of the plot in advance may bring. Some read for the psychological insight such studies bring. Dumas suggested that we read such stories to satisfy a kind of 'egotistical pity'. We end up by thanking God that we are not as other men are, or by saying: 'That's one thing I can't be blamed for'.

Some people read the detective story because they find in it a certain release from anxiety. In it the forces of law and order always win, the crime is always brought home to the culprit, honesty is vindicated. On the not-so-good side, the detective story gives us the chance to act as judge.

Erik Routley holds that the detective story is a product of the Puritan tradition, which is associated with (i) commerce and the values of the city, (ii) rationalism and suspicion of the supernatural, (iii) the assumption that work is a virtue and idleness a vice, (iv) the cult of masculinity, (v) the relegation of sex to a subordinate place in the scheme of human values, exemplified not least in the commendation of late marriage for men, (vi) a special love of good conversation, with which are allied xenophobia, Englishness, a suspicion of artists, and a profound fear of the young. And since the Puritan tradition is on the way out, Dr. Routley feels that the detective story may well be on the way out too. But I do not think that that will happen, so long as there are enough of us who read these stories for no better reason than that we like them.

Here Barclay has come upon a most unusual subject for review. Doctor Routley, the learned hymnologist, has set out to demonstrate the rather unlikely proposition that detective stories are a product of the Puritan tradition. Barclay reveals that he himself is a detective story addict as, apparently, have been a surprising number of biblical scholars, including H. Wheeler

[1] Published by VICTOR GOLLANCZ, 1972.

Robinson and A. S. Peake. And he quotes the remarkable opinion held by the author of this book that one of the reasons for the popularity of the detective story in the Puritan tradition was that 'The relegation of sex to a subordinate place in the scheme of human values, exemplified not least in the commendation of late marriage for men'.

THE ELABORATE FUNERAL, MAN, DOOM AND GOD
Gavin Reid

It may be a salutary thing but it is never a pleasing thing to be battered with facts of doom. And that is precisely what Gavin Reid does to us in the first half of this book[1]. There are few books with such a documented account of the way in which mankind is rushing to it doom.

There is the threat of nuclear war. We are living in what can only be called 'a balance of terror'. 'The nuclear stockpiles of the superpowers contain the equivalent of a hundred tons of TNT for every man, woman and child upon the earth.' There now exist bombs with the equivalent of 48,000,000 tons of TNT in them. A one-megaton bomb, that is, a bomb with the explosive power of 1,000,000 tons of TNT will flatten all buildings in an area of 70 square kilometres. Areas within three times that radius will be liable to fire; and on top of that there is the radiation which would kill many of those who survived. Since 1945, it is estimated, the Soviet Union and the United States have between them spent 1,000,000,000,000 dollars on developing nuclear forces.

There is the threat of an overcrowded world. Within two hundred years in 1850 the population had doubled again to 1,000,000,000. In eighty years it had doubled again; and now the doubling-time is about thirty-five years. Add to these facts that the doubling is not uniform, but is fastest in the undeveloped countries which can least afford it. And then add to that that one-fifth of the world's population is well fed, two-fifths are at subsistence level, and two-fifths are starving. If the human race 'is bent on populating itself to death' does compulsory limitation not become an obligation?

Take the case of pollution. 6,000,000,000 practically indestructible plastic bottles are flung out by British housewives every year. Car fumes are so bad that in Los Angeles they blot out the sun, and in Tokyo there are actually slotmachine oxygen vendors on the street to enable people to buy a few breaths of clean air.

Where does the Church stand in relation to the world? The Church has been related to the world in four different ways. It began by being no more than a beach-head in the world. Then in the time of Constantine it reached the stage of acceptance in the world. Then in the middle ages it reached a place of domination in the world—a position which it often sadly misused. Finally, it has come to the second acceptance phase, when no one objects to it, but no one pays any attention to it.

What are the possible attitudes to all this? There can be *resignation*. There is *abdication*, and there is *confrontation*.

The last sentence of the book is a shout of faith. The Christian believes that 'the world will not end with a bang or a whimper. It will end with the triumphant sound of a trumpet—and then all heaven will be let loose!'

In reviewing this book, Barclay makes the valid point that it is never exactly enjoyable to be, as he puts it, 'battered with facts of doom'. He might have added that it was not particularly useful, either. But here he is faced with a volume which does just that. And, if we may add to the doom, it may be said that the general

[1] Published by HODDER & STOUGHTON, 1972.

Doomsday scenario has become even worse since this book was published in 1972. According to some, we are threatened either with nuclear annihilation, atmospheric asphyxiation, or with the general poisoning of our environment. As Barclay rightly makes plain in this piece, for the Christian there can be three possible attitudes to this: resignation, abdication or confrontation. And like the writer of the book, he would appear to have opted for the last. Indeed, his stout Biblical ethic would allow no other.

THE EXPECTATION OF THE POOR, THE CHURCH AND THE THIRD WORLD
B. N. Y. Vaughan

When a well stocked mind combines with a deeply moved heart, then a valuable book is likely to emerge. The subject of this book is the relationship between the developed and the developing countries.

There is no doubt that when the once colonial countries were given their political independence, there arose a neo-colonialism, which issued in an economic dependence which was quite as binding as the previous political dependence. The aid which is given is often given for no other than selfish reasons. The giving of aid was simply a way of enabling—and even forcing—the aided country to buy the products of the aiding country.

This can issue in a situation in which the raw materials of the country aided have to be sold at a lower and lower price, only to be processed by the aiding country at a higher and higher price. It can issue in a situation in which the highest paid people in the developing countries are the expatriate experts who are imported to run the new industries. It can issue in a situation in which foreign machinery is sold to the developing country, which foreign experts have still to run and to maintain. It can issue in a situation in which the aid given has to be spent in such a way as the aiding country insists, so that there can emerge a lunatic situation in which Russia sells snow ploughs to Guinea!

If aid is to be given, it must be given for the sake of the developing country, not simply selfishly for the sake of the giver; and the developing country must be allowed to be really its own master, even if that means making its own mistakes.

One of the most interesting discussions in the book is the discussion of the place of violence in the struggle for freedom. The World Council of Churches at its meeting in Zagorsk declared that 'we must realize that some Christians find themselves in situations where they must, in all responsibility, participate fully in the revolution with all its inevitable violence'. In 1968 at the meeting in Beirut it said that 'as a last resort men's conscience may lead them in full and clear-sighted responsibility without hate or rancour to engage in violent revolution'.

Dr. Vaughan discusses this fully and thoughtfully. It is clear that political revolution is not enough; there must also be economic revolution. Love there must be and peace there must be, but love cannot be love and peace cannot be peace unless they are founded on justice.

Peace, therefore, cannot be simply tranquillity; peace cannot even be only the preservation of order. Peace is not simply the absence of trouble; it is the presence of all that makes for complete welfare. To produce this peace there must be a creative tension in which the problems are faced and discussed and solved.

This is so closely wrought and argued a book that no brief notice can do it justice. It is a book which ought to be read and studied and pondered by all who are interested in the future of the world.

Barclay here finds himself involved with a question which is highly relevant today. This is the issue of to what extent and in what manner the World Council of Churches should be involved

Published by SCM PRESS, 1972.

with revolutionary freedom movements. The dilemma for Christians is acute, and it is not surprising to find Barclay giving it his closest attention. When he says that this 'is a book which ought to be read and studied and pondered by all who are interested in the future of the world', he is surely not understating the importance of this morally difficult subject.

MEMOIRS
W. A. Visser't Hooft

There are some books which are interesting but not important, and there are still more books which are important but not interesting; and when a book combines interest and importance in equal proportions it is a very good book indeed. That is what W. A. Visser't Hooft does.[1]

It is a long book. It is a very important book indeed, for Visser't Hooft was the first secretary-general of the World Council of Churches— general more than secretary some one said—and no man in any country and in any church knows more about the ecumenical movement in all its manifestations.

There is first of all the sheer interest of the number of outstanding men who move across its pages. We hear William Temple quoting Benjamin Jowett's reply when he was asked over the dinner table what he really thought about God: 'That is not really important, what matters is what God thinks about me'. We listen to William Temple himself preaching about God: 'While we deliberate, he reigns; when we decide wisely, he reigns; when we decide foolishly, he reigns; when we serve him in humble loyalty, he reigns; when we serve him self-assertively, he reigns'. We see Karl Barth answering questions at a conference. 'Somebody said we were like pygmies throwing darts at an elephant.' We hear Hendrik Kraemer laying it down: 'We have not to make Christianity acceptable for the world, but an inescapable appeal and inevitable question to the world'. We hear Bonhoeffer being asked during the war what he prayed for and answering: 'Since you ask me, I must say that I pray for the defeat of my country, for I believe that this is the only way in which it can pay for the suffering which it has caused in the world'. We listen to Pope Pius IX saying that Councils go through three periods, 'one of the devil, one of men, and one God'.

Visser't Hooft had a clear sense of the danger of what may be called cheap ecumenism. 'Doctrine divides, but service units.' 'In the region of moral and social questions we desire all Christians begin at once to act together as if they were one body in one visible fellowship. This could be done by all alike without any injury to theological principle.' Such statements may sound fine, but it has to be remembered that 'hearts and hands cannot operate without heads'. And it may be that the most useful conference of all is a conference at which there emerges a deeper understanding of the differences; the target must not be a cheap agreement, but a state in which those who differ do not excommunicate each other, but rather keep on talking to each other. The old debates are not yet finished.

One last quotation—the Patriarch Justinian of Bucharest described the duty of the monks in addition to their social and manual work. They were to intercede 'for those who do not know how to pray, who do not want to pray, who cannot pray, and especially for those who have never prayed'. Truly, a magnificent ideal!

Suffice it to say that no one will ever be able to write the history of the ecumenical movement without reading this book.

This book introduces us to a man who is of great significance as the first Secretary-General of the World Council of Churches. Not always the easiest of men, he was certainly an influential

[1] Published by SCM PRESS, 1973.

and powerful person, who in his day knew just about everybody on the Christian scene. Barclay's review of his memoirs is therefore of sterling interest. It is typical of him to select for us the quotation by William Temple of a remark of Benjamin Jowett: 'that is not really important, what matters is what God thinks about me'.

THE GULAG ARCHIPELAGO
A. Solzhenitsyn

The proverb says that you cannot have too much of a good thing. Alexander Solzhenitsyn's book is a deeply moving document.[1]

By and large the book is about what happens to political prisoners in Russia. There could be 12,000,000 people in prison in Russia at any one time, 6,000,000 of whom are political prisoners. It was the principle that it is worthwhile that 999 just persons should perish, if one genuine political criminal is caught in the net. From 1876 until 1904 486 people were executed in Russia: from 1905 until 1908 2200 were executed. From June 1918 to October 1919 1600 were shot. In 1937–1938 500,000 political criminals and 480,000 habitual criminals were executed.

Arrests could happen anywhere. In 1926 Irma Mendel obtained two tickets for the Bolshoi Theatre through the Comintern. She invited Interrogator Klegel, who at the time was courting her, to come to the theatre with her. They sat through the show very affectionately, and when it was over, he took her straight to prison.

The search of a house at the time of arrest was savage. 'During the arrest of locomotive engineer Inoshin a tiny coffin stood in his room, containing the body of his newly dead child. The "jurists" dumped the child's body out of the coffin and searched it.

Escape can be a bigger hell than arrest. In 1936 a priest Father Irakly went to Alma-Ata to visit some believers there. During his absence they came three times to his Moscow apartment to arrest him. 'When he returned, members of his flock met him at the station and refused to let him go home, and for eight years hid him in one apartment after another. The priest suffered so painfully from this harried life that when he was finally arrested in 1942 he sang hymns of praise to God.'

The tortures of the trials are almost beyond belief. The prisoner's throat would be douched with salt water and then for a day he would be given no water to drink. Sleep would be made impossible for a week at a time. Prisoners would have their head squeezed with iron rings; they would be lowered into baths of acid; they would be trussed up naked to be bitten by ants and bed-bugs. A ram rod heated in a primus stove would be thrust up their anal canal (the 'secret brand').

Justice was perverted. What matters is 'not personal guilt, but social danger'. There is only one position from which to judge, 'class expediency'. The question was, not what a man had done, but what he might do, if he was not shot now. 'We protect ourselves not only against the past, but also against the future.'

It is sometimes demanded: 'Don't dig up the past! Dwell on the past and you'll lose an eye'. But the proverb says: 'Forget the past and you'll lose both eyes'.

Wise things are said in the passing. Engels said that 'there could be no greater tragedy for the working class than to seize political power when it is not ready for it'.

At times this is a book which it is almost unbearable to read. But it had to be written, if only to make sure that these things do not happen again.

We move on now a long way in time from the days of Visser't Hooft. It is a sombre thought that

[1] Published by WM. COLLINS & SONS, 1974.

Solzhenitsyn whose historic book about Stalin's labour camps Barclay here reviews, was almost certainly imprisoned in one when Visser't Hooft and the World Council of Churches were confidently building a better world. Not only the nature, but also the sheer size of the Soviet labour camp régime was in itself astonishing, especially before it was scaled down after Stalin's death. It had, of course, existed for many years, since terror was an avowed weapon of the Bolshevik Revolution. Yet, in spite of books by such authors as Robert Conquest, there were many in the West who were reluctant to believe the reality of it. After this book of Solzhenitsyn, such scepticism became ridiculous. Here is the grim truth. As Barclay rightly says 'at times this is a book which is almost unbearable to read'.

INDIA: THE SPEECHES AND REMINISCENCES OF IDIRA GANDHI, PRIME MINISTER OF INDIA
I. Gandhi

The problems of governing a nation are always acute, but what must they be when the nation has 550,000,000 inhabitants, 560,000 villages, 16 major languages, 7 major religions, when time has moved so slowly in it that as late as 1950 there was at least one district in it the inhabitants of which had never used or even seen a wheel? That is India, and something of India's problems and ideals are to be seen in this book.[1]

Although not related to him Mrs. Gandhi knew the Mahatma well. The Mahatma had a mind as wide as the world. 'I do not want', he said, 'my house to be walled in on all sides and my windows to be stuffed. I want the cultures of all lands to be blown about my house as freely as possible, but I refuse to be blown off my feet by any of them. Mine is not a religion of the prison house; it has room for the least among God's creations, but it is proof against the insolent pride of race, religion or colour.' Gandhi was a great leader, but he was identified with the people he led. 'He was the crest of the wave, but they (the people) were the wave itself.'

On two matters especially Mrs. Gandhi has something of the greatest interest to say. The first is what she calls secularism, that secularism which was at the heart of Gandhi's belief and which is at the heart of hers.

The second thing of very great interest and importance is Mrs. Gandhi's conception of democracy. 'The divine right of the people, which is enshrined in democracy, also requires that the will of the people be expressed through reflection and judgment. . . It is not only the water but the banks which make the river. . . Nor by any means can the street be the place where the laws are made. The mob is thus a negation of democracy.' It is not hard to see how such an idea of democracy could at times issue in a benevolent dictatorship.

Mrs. Gandhi is equally interesting on the subject of education. 'Education in the widest sense of the word is the training of mind and body, so as to produce a balanced personality, which is capable of adjusting, without undue disturbance, to life's changing situations.' Mrs. Gandhi believes that it is important to teach a man to read, but it is still more important to see that he reads the right things, when he can read.

Unquestionably the government of India can point to its achievements. In the 1940s the average expectation of life was under 30; it is now $47\frac{1}{2}$. 45,000,000 more children are in schools; 30,000,000 jobs have been created; agricultural production has been almost doubled; there are 2,500,000 students in colleges; at an election, even in the villages, 60% of the people use their vote.

Every now and then Mrs. Gandhi drops memorable sayings. It was Gandhi's greatness that he made heroes out of clay. Tagore wrote: 'Every child comes with the message that God is not discouraged of man'. Radhakrishnan advised the nation 'not to be prisoners of the past but pilgrims of the future'.

This is a very important book which anyone who wishes even to begin to understand India must read.

[1] Published by HODDER & STOUGHTON, 1975.

105

Who would have thought that the Indira Gandhi, whose book Barclay reviews here, could have come to preside for a time over an authoritarian and oppressive régime and then to be politically defeated in the Indian election of 1977? Yet such has been the case. Indira, daughter of the great Nehru, friend of the Mahatma himself, was at the heart of that group of gifted people who were the creators of modern India. In the eyes of the liberal West they could do no wrong. Mrs. Gandhi herself could write, 'the divine right of the people, which is enshrined in democracy, also requires that the will of the people be expressed through reflection and judgement . . .' Perhaps they had time for both when they were in prison. 'This', as Barclay says, 'is a very important book.' It is also, at this distance of time, a sad one.

ENCOUNTER WITH MARTIN BUBER
Aubrey Hodes

Aubrey Hodes has given us an intensely interesting book.[1] Martin Buber will always be known as the man who drew the distinction between the I, thou and it relationship with other people. The I–thou relationship means relating to people with the whole of our being. It means a genuine encounter, a reciprocal relationship which puts the I in tune with life. The I–it relationship implies treating the other person not as a person but as an object, a thing to be used and to be thought of not as a subject on the same level as oneself.

Buber summed up his philosophy of life in the saying: 'All real living is meeting'. And we either meet the other person as a person, as a thou to whom we respond with our whole personality, or we meet him as a thing of which we want to make use. John Robinson in expounding this idea took the example of a chimney-sweep coming to his house:

I meet him as the possessor of a chimney that is full of soot; he meets me as one who is skilled in removing that soot. Apart from that we might never have met, and the chances are that my contact with him will be limited strictly to the transaction of sweeping.

That is the I–it relationship. The I–thou relationship is distinctively personal; the I–it relationship is 'functional and instrumental'.

It is precisely in our love for our neighbour that we meet God. Buber hears God say: 'You think I am far away from you; but in your love for your neighbour you will find me—not in his love for you but in yours for him'.

'Existence will remain meaningless for you if you yourself do not penetrate into it with active love and if you do not in this way discover its meaning for yourself. Everything is waiting to be hallowed by you ... Meet the world with the fullness of your being and you shall meet God. If you wish to believe, love!'

Thus there can be no higher activity than loving help to our fellow men, a truth contained in Isaac Loeb Peretz's story 'If not higher': A rabbi disappeared from the Synagogue for a few hours every Day of Atonement. One of his followers suspects that he is secretly meeting the Almighty, and follows him. He watches as the rabbi puts on coarse peasant clothes and cares for an invalid woman in a cottage, cleaning out her room and preparing food for her. The follower goes back to the Synagogue and when he is asked, 'Did the rabbi ascend to heaven?', he replies, 'If not higher'.

Mr. Hodes deals with many aspects of the teaching of Martin Buber out of loving personal knowledge of the man. The book is the book not only of a man who knew and admired Buber's teaching, but who knew and loved Buber. Buber said that man in our time was being polarized between the two extremes of individualism and collectivism, and both were wrong. Individualism understands only a part of man, but collectivism understands man only as a part. The real way to find man is in community, and Mr. Hodes was very much a member of that community of which Martin Buber was the centre.

Any reviewer faces an easier task when he has before him a book about happenings rather than a book about

[1] Published by ALAN LANE, 1972; PENGUIN BOOKS, 1976.

ideas. With this volume concerning the distinguished philosopher-theologian, Martin Buber, Barclay is clearly faced with a book fitting into the second category. There was nothing simple about Buber, and it is a testimony to Barclay's capacity for interpretation and clarification, that he can produce a readable review of a notoriously difficult subject. In passing, we might add that it throws light on the essentially community-orientated teaching of Barclay, which underpins his doctrine of the church and ecumenicity.

III The things of God

THE MODERN RIVAL OF CHRISTIAN FAITH
Georgia Harkness

In the Pastoral Epistles Paul is represented as saying 'I suffer not a woman to teach' (1 Ti 2¹²). Perhaps even Paul would have made an exception to his prohibition if he had read this book.¹ Dr. Harkness is Professor of Applied Theology at the Pacific School of Religion and obviously she is a born teacher.

The book is a discussion of secularism and it falls into three parts—Secularism and the Christian Faith, Rival Secular Faiths, and The Way Forward. Dr. Harkness has certain characteristics as a writer. First, she has absolute fairness of mind. Second, she has an extraordinary power of lucid analysis of a situation or a theory. Third, she has a unique gift for producing definitions which are helpful and stimulating.

She lists four things as essential to Christianity. (*a*) An act of commitment to Jesus Christ. (*b*) That act of commitment which issues in a real attempt to live by the example and teaching of Jesus Christ. (*c*) A belief in God the Father and in the Divinity of Jesus. (*d*) Membership of the universal Church.

She lists four types of Christians who are to be found within the Church. (i) The person of warm Christian devotion who does not think very much of his theology and lives his religion as he understands it. (ii) Those who take their religion pretty casually. Secularism has already sucked the vitality from their religion. (iii) The dogmatically opinionated fundamentalist, who believes with no questions asked. (iv) The open-minded seeker who is eager to know what he can believe and what he can teach his children.

If we are to fulfil Christ's command to go and teach all nations, Dr. Harkness believes that we need three things. (*a*) We must have a closer union of evangelism with education.

(*b*) We must have a closer union of Christian experience with Christian belief; that is, we need more and better theology. (*c*) We need a much closer union of Sunday religion with the day's work.

But the really unique character of the book is its passion for definition and its success therein. 'Secularism is the ordering of life as if God did not exist.' 'Scientism is an exclusive devotion to the methods and procedures of science in a way that rules out other legitimate and necessary devotions such as those implied in the Christian faith.' Democracy as an ethical ideal 'means a recognition of the intrinsic worth of every person with the corresponding right of every person to the fullest possible self-realisation.' 'Racism is assumption of biological and social superiority by a dominant group on the basis of actual or alleged differences in race or colour.' Destiny is the conviction that 'something lies ahead which bears a significant relation to the present.'

'Jesus counselled trustful waiting but never inertia about the Kingdom.'

There are few better books on the modern situation than this. For wise sanity of thinking and lucidity of writing it is outstanding.

Here again Barclay is concerned with a book of ideas. What is more, it is a book emanating from an area of American scholarship where theology and sociology sometimes combine in such a way as does not always lead to clarity of expression. But it is clear

Published by ABINGDON-COKESBURY PRESS.

that Barclay found none of these difficulties in this book. He ascribes to its writer three characteristics which are also markedly his own: absolute fairness of mind, an extraordinary power of lucid analysis, and a supreme gift for producing definitions which are both helpful and stimulating. It also demonstrates Barclay's early and undeviating position regarding the position of women (it is one of his earliest reviews)!

A FAITH TO PROCLAIM
J. S. Stewart

It has been said, and said truly, that there can be no preaching without passion. Professor James S. Stewart, D.D., is one of the very greatest of present-day preachers. In his preaching the dominant note is intensity and it is his supreme gift as a writer than, even in the printed word, he can convey that passionate intensity of belief. He has already given us one volume on preaching, his Warrack Lectures 'Heralds of God'; and now we have from his pen this one.[1]

As the title shows the book is concerned not with the technique and methods but with the subject and content of preaching. The preacher's task today is 'to confront a bewildered and dishevelled age with the fact of Christ.' Apostolic preaching was very far from 'that familiar blend of legalism, humanitarian sentiment, and cosmopolitan toleration which sometimes in this twentieth century passes for religion'. The book has five chapters entitled, 'Proclaiming the Incarnation', 'Proclaiming Forgiveness', 'Proclaiming the Cross', 'Proclaiming the Resurrection', and 'Proclaiming Christ'.

Let us see what Dr. Stewart has to say about proclaiming forgiveness. He asks three questions. First, *'Is forgiveness necessary?'* A man may say, 'There is some mistake! Christ has come to the wrong address. . . . That is not troubling me!' Such a man does not believe 'in the reality of sin.' 'No cumulation', said Reinhold Niebuhr, 'of contradictory evidence seems to disturb modern man's good opinion of himself.' What then are 'God's ways of piercing the armour?' A man may be driven to recognize sin by *'the chaos of the world'*. He may be driven to recognize it by *'the character of Christ'*.

Second, Dr. Stewart asks, *'Is forgiveness possible?'* Can anything break the law of cause and effect? 'Take what you will, said God, take it—and pay for it', says the Spanish proverb. First, we must remember that forgiveness is neither the remission of penalty or consequence but *the restoration of a relationship*. It is to say, as Bengel said, 'O God, there is nothing between us.' Second, there is *'the actual testimony of the forgiven'*. Third, there is the fact that we are dealing with *'the God and Father of our Lord Jesus Christ'*.

The third question Dr. Stewart asks is, *'Is forgiveness right?'* There are three answers. First, God forgives but never makes light of sin. As Denney said, 'To take the condemnation out of the Cross is to take the nerve out of the Gospel'. Second, forgiveness does not demoralize a man, it has precisely the opposite effect. It reduces him to a gratitude which passionately tries to deserve it. Third, God's method was *'to redeem the whole sinful situation'*. In Christ and the Cross there came 'a force capable of shattering for the first time that vicious circle in which the human race was bound and helpless'.

Finally, Dr. Stewart lays it down that all the why and how and the wherefore of this need not necessarily be understood; the radiant thing is that it can be appropriated.

Dr. Stewart does not argue; he states things with passion. If it be true that preaching is witnessing then this is preaching at its best.

Readers of Barclay's own autobiography Testament of Faith

[1] Published by HODDER & STOUGHTON, 1963.

will remember with what awe and respect he writes of preaching: 'for me to enter a pulpit has always been a literally terrifying experience. . . All my life I have regarded preaching with dread'. It is therefore all the more interesting to read how Barclay deals with it. He fairly and lucidly describes the major features of the writer's message.

Whether he agrees with it all—and his own words in Testament of Faith on preaching in general may usefully be compared with what he has to say here—is another matter. He ends with a characteristic question 'If it be true that preaching is witnessing, then this is preaching at its best'.

THE REDISCOVERY OF THE BIBLE
W. Neil

Of the making of books about the Bible there is no end and it is well that it should be so. This book[1] is written to help people who wish to make that attempt. Dr. Neil is well aware that, apart from those who would like to read the Bible and who cannot, there are those who are actively opposed to the Bible. There is need to commend the Bible today both to those who have laid it aside because they can make nothing of it, and to those who have laid it aside because they think it a relic of an outworn past.

Dr. Neil places his finger on the spot when he says: 'One of the most disconcerting features in any branch of knowledge is the time-lag between the promulgation of new ideas in the scholar's study and the assimilation of these ideas by the man in the street'. There is no doubt whatever that there has been far too little of a teaching ministry through which the discoveries of scholars could be brought to lay people. It is true that new knowledge is often suspect and resented. But Dr. Neil reminds us of the words of Erasmus: 'By identifying the new learning with heresy we make orthodoxy synonymous with ignorance'. It is also true that the 'new learning' has often been presented with a certain arrogant destructiveness which did antagonize simple people, but that is a fault from which Dr. Neil is completely free.

In this book Dr. Neil does two great things. First, he brings to the ordinary reader the results of up-to-date scholarship and he brings them always in a positive form. He is not concerned so much to contradict and belittle the old, as he is to inculcate the new. Second, he gives us a wide, sweeping view of the Bible story and purpose. The trouble about detailed study of the Bible is that very often it prevents the student from seeing the Bible as a whole. Dr. Neil gives the Bible reader a key and scheme which enables him to see the Bible as a whole. 'In one sense it [the Bible] may be described as a divine-drama, in which are set forth the acts of God in history, seen against a back-cloth of eternity. There are a prologue (Genesis 1–2), an epilogue (the Book of Revelation), and three acts. The first act tells of the Call and Failure of Israel, the second act records the Coming of Christ, and the third act the Foundation of the Christian Church.' If a man set out to read the Bible like that, it would open out like a drama before him. Dr. Neil well reminds us that 'In ancient times people were not concerned as we are today about any story of this kind: Is it true? Did it really happen? They rather asked: What is the point of the story? What is it meant to teach?' It may fitly be said that Dr. Neil's book enables us better to understand *the point of the Bible*. In the Bible we find that 'Word from Beyond for our human predicament'. That is why we read it.

It is now twenty years since this book was first published. Not the least interesting feature of this review is that it concerns a book which was the debut of the writer upon the scene of Biblical interpretation. Dr. Neil, for many years of the University of Nottingham, has had much to give to that scene ever since. His One Volume Commentary on the Bible, *to name but one of his many subsequent books, is still in a class by itself. Barclay is at his best here, as is often*

[1] Published by HODDER & STOUGHTON, 1958.

the case when he is reviewing a book
about the Bible. And he praises
William Neil for two things which
he has himself for so long done so well:
'he brings to the ordinary reader the
results of up-to-date scholarship,
and he gives us a wide, sweeping view
of the Bible's story and purpose.

JESUS OF PALESTINE: THE LOCAL BACKGROUND TO THE GOSPEL DOCUMENTS
Eric F. F. Bishop

It always makes the very greatest difference to know the background against which any event happened. And that is particularly true of the events of the gospel story. For that reason books which tell us of the background of life in Palestine are always interesting, and when they are written out of first-hand and expert knowledge they become of first-rate importance.

This is such a book.[1] Before Mr. Bishop became Lecturer in Arabic in Glasgow University he was for twenty-five years engaged in missionary service in Palestine, and he calls his book 'notes of twentieth-century parallels in thought, speech and action to first-century life in Palestine, as it is depicted to us in the gospel documents'. Mr. Bishop goes consecutively through the gospel narrative citing such parallels as he goes.

In a book like this we can only dip at random, and every time we emerge with treasure-trove. Mk I[13] speaks of Jesus being alone with the wild beasts in the wilderness during His temptation. 'The root of the word used for wild animals in Arabic—*wuhūsh*—carries the implication both of desolation, loneliness and the withdrawal from human ·society. Today, when a friend returns after a long absence, the greeting is heard—*awashtana*—you have made us feel like wild animals for loneliness'.

Jesus invited men to take His yoke upon them and to learn of Him (Mt 11[29-30]). 'The Palestinian yoke is always meant for two.' When a young ox is broken in, it is always yoked beside 'an older one, accustomed to the work', and thus the younger one learns to bear the yoke.

Many of the strong vivid terms of the gospel will be illuminated if we remember that in Eastern language 'There are no middle terms between "doing good" and "doing evil", between "saving life" and destroying it'. 'There is no middle term between black and white. Grey is not reckoned as a colour.'

There is one very interesting note on the way in which salt might be cast out and trodden underfoot of men. 'Miss F. E. Newton suggests that the reference is to ovens built of stone and tiles. In these "in order to retain the heat a thick bed of salt is laid under the tiled floor. After a certain length of time the salt perishes. The tiles are taken up, the salt removed and thrown into the road outside the door of the oven. . . It has lost its power to heat the tiles, so it has been thrown out".'

Mr. Bishop quotes a modern instance to illustrate the Parable of the Guest without the Garment. 'When some members of the Anglo-American Committee of Enquiry visited the King of Sa'ūdi Arabia in 1946, they were presented among other things with Arab dress; which in any case it would have been courteous to wear, though unlikely that westerners might possess.'

There is not a page in this fascinating book which does not help the New Testament to come alive.

Once again concerned with the field of Biblical interpretation, Barclay is breathing, one could say, his own air. His own book The First Three Gospels *appeared long after this particular book on the background of the Gospel documents was written. But readers of that book can see why*

[1] Published by LUTTERWORTH PRESS, 1956.

this one has particular interest for Barclay, since it is concerned with shedding contemporary light on the Gospel documents. Barclay's lengthy

quotation here of a comment on the phrase 'the salt has lost its savour' is an illustration of his own appetite for this kind of helpful observation.

AN ARROW INTO THE AIR
J. H. Withers

Each age has had its own special problems of communication; and therefore each age has had to evolve its own technique of communication. Our own age has had to evolve one quite new technique—the technique of the broadcast sermon. That that technique is of the greatest importance is beyond a doubt, when we remember that a service like the People's Service has a listening public of over ten million listeners. Mr. Withers is one of that select band of preachers who has been, in the highest sense, outstandingly successful both in the pulpit and on the air.[1]

Mr. Withers has no mean conception of preaching. 'The sermon—ideally at least—is the prophetic application of the Word of Holy Scripture to the needs and tendencies of today. . .

When we study these sermons we find that they combine two elements in their technique—clarity in their construction, and vividness in their illustration. The volume begins with a sermon on 'Stress and Strain' with Ex 18^{23} in the Moffatt translation as a text: 'If you do this, then you can stand the strain'. First, there is *Relaxation through Prayer*. William James has an essay entitled 'The Energies of Men'. In it he quotes Dr. Hyslop, a famous specialist in diseases of the mind as saying that 'the best sleep-provoking agent which his practice had revealed to him was prayer. I say this, he added, purely as a medical man. The exercise of prayer must be regarded by us doctors as the most adequate and normal of the pacifiers of the mind and calmers of the nerves'. Second there is *Resignation from Unnecessary Responsibility*. Hezekiah knew the technique of peace when he took the threatening letter and spread it out before the Lord. Once when Bishop

Quayle was lying awake one night worrying, he heard God say to him: 'Quayle, you go to sleep; I'll sit up for the rest of the night'. Third, there is *Recreation through Worship*. The head of a large hospital had an exhausting time during an epidemic, when her staff was short. 'One day she said to a subordinate: "I'm all in. I must consult a nerve specialist or"—and she did not know why she said it—"or else go to Church".' She did go to Church and there she found her peace.

Again and again Mr. Withers seizes on the memorable quotation. Aldous Huxley defined our modern progress as: 'Improved means for unimproved ends'. William Temple said that it was as if a burglar had broken into the world's shop; but, instead of stealing the articles for sale, he changed the price tickets, so that the goods which are really valuable are marked at a cheap price, and the shoddy, worthless things suddenly appeared very expensive and highly desirable.

There is in this book skill in unforgettable sermon construction, width and catholicity in the selection of illustrative material, combined with patent sincerity. There is gospel in these sermons, and that is no doubt the reason why the arrow in them did not fall uselessly to earth but lodged its truth in some one's heart.

Once again we are reminded by this review of how seriously Barclay has always regarded the duty and the privilege of preaching. We may also be reminded of how well he has been

[1] Published by JAMES CLARK, 1958.

able to use the radio as a vehicle for his own teaching. With the growth of Local Radio, this book is by no means out of date, and it is good that a veteran braodcaster should himself be reviewed by one of proven talents in that field.

STRENGTHENING THE SPIRITUAL LIFE
Nels D. S. Ferré

There are not a few men who possess great scholarship, and there are not a few men who possess great depth of spiritual life, but there are very few men who can communicate something of their own greatness and their own experience to others. Professor Nels F. S. Ferré is such a man. His book[1] is not a long book; but no one will put it down without a clearer idea of what the spiritual life is, and of practical means towards strengthening it.

Professor Ferré tells how his wife had a dream that she had to write an essay on 'How to Stop Worrying'. In the dream she was able to write an inspired flow of words; but when she awoke she could remember only the three points of the outline: 'Worship, work and wait'. That, says Professor Ferré, is the Divine formula for all who need relief from worry. He goes on to expand it.

Professor Ferré has a wonderful chapter on *Personal Devotions* and on private prayer. This chapter is full of wise counsel. 'The first rule of prayer is to learn *relaxation*.' 'God has made the world self-defeating for the self-serious.' It is better to pray lying down than to kneel in stiff discomfort, although there are times when a man's first instinct is to kneel. There must be spiritual relaxation as well as physical relaxation. Next there comes *recollection*. This involves the recalling of who God is. 'He is both ultimate reality and our most intimate friend.' It is only a pagan who needs to bow and scrape and plead before his god. But we must also recollect that 'God loves everyone completely.' And, therefore, we cannot pray selfishly, but only when we are 'surrendered to the common good'. Prayer is *communion*. There must therefore be in it quietness, that there may not only be speech, but the silence of listening, and of that communion which is beyond even listening. Prayer begins with *adoration* which is 'the self's finding reality and rest'. It is that in which we understand a 'fragment of the future'. *Adoration* will immediately overflow into gratitude; and intercession and petition for service will pour out along with thanksgiving.

It is but natural that Professor Ferré should have a section on the reading of the Bible. It must be read *slowly*, never skimmed. It must be read *devotionally*, but that does not mean parking the mind outside. Some time must be spent in '*dwelling with the great saints of the Church*'. And there must be *study*. The best stimulus to keep going is a partner or a group with whom we discuss that which we read.

We have said nothing about the loveliest chapter in the book—the chapter on 'Family Worship'. This whole book is the outcome of personal experience.

Professor Ferré's experience of life has given him the right to speak, for he himself is not only one of life's scholars; he is also one of life's victors. The only real authority is the authority of personal experience, and from this book of rare beauty that authority breathes forth.

Barclay obviously enjoyed reviewing what he describes as a 'book of rare beauty'. That is not surprising, given the deep personal experience with which he writes. Typically, Barclay manages to extract a telling story. Ferré's wife had a dream that she had to write an essay on 'how to stop worrying'.

[1] Published by WM. COLLINS & SONS, 1956.

Awaking, she could remember only three points about a possible outline 'worship, work and wait'. That, as the writer points out, is the divine formula for all who need relief from worry. Those— *and they are many—who have benefited from the even tenor of Barclay's own writings, which seem so often to speak of an inner tranquility, will particularly value this anecdote.*

THROUGH GATES OF SPLENDOUR
Elisabeth Elliot

The Acts of the Apostles can never be a finished volume, but must always be a continued story; another chapter in these Acts has been told by Elisabeth Elliot.[1] Few more thrilling missionary stories have ever been told; and in this case the interest of the story is made many times more vivid by magnificent photographs of Cornell Capa.

In the early 1950's five young men, all connected with Faith-Missions, and their wives, were converging on the missionary task in Ecuador.

There was Jim Elliot, honours student, champion wrestler, amateur poet, most popular of students and convinced Christian. In his diary, during his college days, he writes: ' "He makes His ministers a flame of fire." Am I ignitible? God deliver me from the dread asbestos of "other things". Saturate me with the oil of the Spirit that I may be a flame'. He knew that he must go to Ecuador. 'I am as sure of His direction,' he said, 'as I am of His salvation.'

There was Peter Fleming, distinguished student in philosophy and literature, who might well have become a college professor if he had chosen the easy way.

There was Nate Saint, flying-mad from his boyhood, kept from a career in the Air Force, distinguished as a ground engineer, and with a flair for all kinds of gadgets and inventions. He became a pilot with the Missionary Aviation Fellowship, the MAF, and with the little yellow Piper aircraft, with its two-way wireless, was the greatest ally missionaries could have. He had the caution of the expert, and the recklessness of the disciple.

There was Ed McCully, six feet two, one hundred and ninety pounds of him. He was an athlete of the most extraordinary determination.

There was Roger Youderian, the victim of polio, yet a decorated paratrooper at the Battle of the Bulge in 1944.

These young men and their wives worked amongst the Jivaros and the Quichuas; but one tribe haunted them. That tribe was the Aucas, a primitive tribe of killers, their ferocity increased by the reckless brutality of the rubber traders between 1875 and 1925, a tribe absolutely untouched by any word from Christ.

They laid their plans. Everything was done. By use of the Piper aircraft they established some kind of contact with the Aucas. They learned some few phrases: 'I like you! I am your friend! I like you!' These phrases they shouted down by loud-speaker. They developed a clever system of dropping the Aucas gifts from the aeroplane at the end of a spiral line. They even got the length of having the Aucas send them up gifts at the end of the line by which their gifts were dropped. They never forgot that the Aucas were killers.

Then they dropped in on a strip of sand and waited for the Aucas to come. They were able to communicate with their headquarters with their two-way wireless set. But there was silence. What happened no one will ever know; but when a rescue party was flown in all that was left was the dead bodies of these five gallant adventurers for Christ.

The strange thing about this book is that it ought to be read as a tragedy, humanly speaking, and somehow it reads as a triumph. And the heroism of the young widows who are left is even greater than the heroism of the young men who died, for it is the greatest of all heroisms, the heroism of going on.

[1] Published by HODDER & STOUGHTON, 1957.

It was the young widow of one of the missionaries who wrote this celebrated book which Barclay here reviews. His concluding observation is well worth remembering; that more was required of those who were bereaved than those who were killed; because it was the bereaved who had to keep going on.

POWER IN PREACHING
W. E. Sangster

People who are experts both in theory and in practice are rare. For one man who can *show* us how to do it there are a hundred men who can *tell* us how to do it. The great characteristic of Dr. W. E. Sangster is that he is a master of both the theory and the practice of preaching.[1]

Dr. Sangster is fully aware of the difficulty of the present situation. He quotes certain facts given by Admiral Sir Geoffrey Layton in a speech at Portsmouth. A simple examination in religious knowledge was set to young men joining the Navy. They were a fair cross-section of the population, if anything of rather higher than average intelligence. Only twenty-three per cent could repeat the Lord's Prayer accurately; twenty-eight per cent knew it in part; forty-nine per cent knew no more than the opening words. Seventy-two per cent knew who Jesus Christ was, but only thirty-nine per cent knew where He was born. What happened on Good Friday was known to sixty-two per cent, but only forty-five per cent knew about Easter, and only one man in forty could explain Whitsuntide. There is the situation.

Dr. Sangster enumerates six different kinds of preaching—Bible Interpretation, Ethical and Devotional, Doctrinal, Philosophic and Apologetic, Social, Evangelistic. But he is open-eyed to the faults in present-day preaching. 'A Christian man talking in a pulpit with an open Bible in front of him is not necessarily preaching the gospel.' 'All the evidence goes to show that a great deal of Protestant preaching for a generation past has been on marginal things.' The danger is that preachers attempt 'the impossible task of making a staple diet out of sugary trifles.' The topical sermon has its dangers.

Dr. Sangster recalls men to the great purposes of preaching: 'Here, then, is the preacher's task: to preach about God, to show man his own real nature, to expose sin, to announce the way of salvation, to stagger people with the truth of the Incarnation, to hold up in a hundred ways the truth of the Atonement, to tell of the work of the Holy Spirit, and to proclaim all the refinements of grace'. One of the great failures of preaching is to answer the question *how*? Even the greatest things must be stated with clarity.

Dr. Sangster never forgets that prayer is the dynamic at the back of all great preaching. He tells of the negro preacher who said that he 'read himself full', then 'thought himself clear', and finally 'prayed himself hot', indeed an ideal recipe for preaching.

Sometimes his impatience with the lack of lucidity takes him too far. 'If the teaching is so abstruse that it simply cannot be made plain to plain people, it may be doubted whether it belongs to the Gospel once delivered to the saints.' There is truth there—but it is dangerous doctrine, for there is nothing so perilous as over-simplification.

Any preacher will rise from the reading of this book humbled, challenged, abashed and inspired— and that is exactly the effect a book on preaching should have.

Earlier in this volume (p. 17) we found Barclay reviewing a biography of the celebrated Methodist preacher, the late Doctor Sangster, written by his son. Here we find him concerned with a work

[1] Published by EPWORTH PRESS, 1958.

125

by Dr. Sangster himself, on a subject which was at the very heart of Sangster's ministry. Without a doubt, he was a very great exponent of this art, and practised at a time when its appeal was probably greater than now. But the preaching of the word will always be an essential part of a Christian ministry, and no one is more aware of this than Barclay.

RELIGIOUS EXPERIENCE
A. E. Baker

It is something to meet a man who was interested in the arts, a great reader of poetry, very knowledgeable on painting, a provocative writer on the method and the meaning of tragedy, with a competent appreciation of music, a master of metaphysics, with understanding of the principles and aims of natural science a lecturer equally at home with Plato, Browning or Christian theology, a successful diocesan bishop, a first-class chairman, and 'a very good listener with a ready laugh which put most people at their ease', an energetic Church reformer, with a sensitive interest in and understanding of ordinary people. Such a man was William Temple. Canon A. E. Baker has collected certain essays and addresses of William Temple, under this title.[1]

The titles of these essays and addresses show the width and the grasp of William Temple's mind; but Canon Baker has added infinitely to the value and the worth of this book by his sympathetic and penetrating study of William Temple himself.

It was Temple's achievement that, as the journalists put it, 'He put Christianity on the map'.

He was a man of sturdy commonsense. 'He believed that when a decision had to be taken one should say one's prayers putting before God all the aspects of the matter so far as one understood them, and then, one should make up one's mind and act on it; and never waste time afterwards in vain regrets.'

No man had a greater social consciousness. 'Temple took for granted that Christianity is concerned, not only with the salvation of individuals, but also with the transformation of the social order.'

He was of all men most tolerant. At his enthronement in York he said: 'We shall strive for the truth as we see it, but shall never suppose that there is no truth but what we have seen'. He called on men to lay all partisanship aside and to become 'partisans of good will'.

Not unnaturally he was an apostle of real unity between the churches. In this matter he had three principles. (1) There are divisions within the Church, but these divisions do not effect separation from the Church. He insisted that when he prayed for 'the Church' he was praying for every conceivable branch of the Church. (2) 'Faith and order are not equally essential.' He did not believe that there was any one necessary order. (3) In any meetings concerned with unity he believed that those taking part should be more eager to appropriate what was of value in the position of others than to justify their own.

The most characteristic thing about William Temple was his passionate belief in the Incarnation. For him 'the central fundamental affirmation of the Christian religion is that Jesus of Nazareth is the unique, final manifestation of God'.

William Temple, being dead, yet speaks. We are grateful to Canon Baker for collecting these essays and addresses; we are still more grateful to him that in his loving Preface he has made William Temple live again.

Canon Baker of York was a keen student of William Temple, and a devoted collater and assembler of his works. It is clear that Barclay, in company with many other Christians,

[1] Published by JAMES CLARK, 1958.

admired Temple and felt enriched by him. He is therefore clearly grateful to Canon Baker for this collection of some essays and addresses of Temple who, as Barclay says, 'being dead yet speaks', and the things of which he speaks, and which are demonstrated in this notice, are those which have characterized Barclay's teaching and ministry, namely, sturdy common-sense, social concern, tolerance, ecumenical concern and devotion—beyond all other matters—to the final revelation of God in Jesus Christ.

THIS WORLD AND BEYOND
R. Bultmann

There are few things more interesting than to read the sermons of a great and controversial theologian, if for no other reason than to see if he keeps his technical theology and his ordinary preaching in separate compartments. We will, therefore, obviously turn to the sermons of Professor Rudolf Bultmann with the greatest interest.[1]

These are first and foremost the sermons of a man who loves the Bible. At the beginning of one sermon Professor Bultmann quotes the words of Matthias Claudius: 'The words of Christ are like a fountain which never dries up. When you draw from this fountain of wisdom, it fills up again, and the second truth you derive is fuller and more splendid than the first.'

It will be best to test this volume at a point where, if we may put it so, Bultmann can be most characteristically Bultmann. We, therefore, turn to the sermon on Lk 5^{1-10}, on the miraculous catch of fishes, for here we find set out the Bultmann conception of miracle.

As things are today, we are both theoretically and practically convinced that events happen according to certain fixed laws, and according to natural cause and effect. We are quite aware that there are certain things beyond immediate comprehension, but these things are under the constant investigation of the human mind.

As Professor Bultmann sees it, 'Belief in the miracle stories of the New Testament is not in fact the essence of the Christian faith. Christian faith means rather faith in the grace of God which has been manifested in Christ'. There are some who claim that, since everything must be surrendered to Christ, then our intellect too must be surrendered; but it can never be a Christian duty to sin against the truth, as a man sees the truth.

In the story of this passage under discussion Bultmann frankly sees 'a pious fiction'. The point of the story is that the sinful Peter is to become a fisher of men; the real miracle is the choice of Peter for this task and the effectiveness of the divine Word on human lips.

Must, then, the conception of the miraculous go? Certainly not! Man's refusal to believe in the miraculous, and man's insistence on law, is due to man's sinful desire for independence, for a universe which he thinks he can control, for his refusal to accept his total dependence on God.

The real miracle is the miracle of creation, not creation in the sense of the creation of the world, but the creation of *me*. As Luther had it, to believe in God the Creator is to believe that 'God has created *me* together with all other creatures', a belief which, Luther goes on to say, 'few people have progressed so far as to believe in the fullest sense'. If God has created *me*, it means that all life is in the hands of God. Can we hold that faith when we are apparently 'struck by a fate which threatens to break us utterly'? Can we hold it 'in hours of cruel pain and bitterest renunciation and sacrifice'? If we really and truly hold this unshakable belief in God the Creator then miracle essentially means that we become profoundly and constantly aware that this is not a closed and shut universe but that 'in spite of everything, in spite of all the mysteries of the world and destiny, in spite of the torment of our self-condemnation, God has created us by His grace, and holds us in His Creator's hand'.

[1] Published by LUTTERWORTH PRESS.

The true meaning of the miracle story of the catch of fishes is that God comes to us when we admit that we have come to the end of our resources and that in that moment He calls sinful man to His service, and recreates him and renews him for His service, for that is precisely what happened to Peter. God's miraculous power comes into life always when we stop trying to shape life for ourselves and submit to Him, the Creator of life.

There is little doubt that this is the most significant book of sermons that has appeared for many a long day.[1] They are very long; they are sometimes anything but easy, but again and again they return to the basic conception of the inadequacy of man and the triumphant adequacy of God.

To many the very name of Bult-mann is an offence, but let them read this truly great book and surely they will be left saying: 'Should such a faith offend?'

To many, as Barclay comments, 'the very name of Bultmann is an offence,' although he makes it clear that he is not one of them. Even so, he must have felt considerable curiosity as to how this great radical theologian, the pioneer demythologiser in New Testament criticism, would combine that aspect of his life and work with that of his calling as a Christian Minister. As Barclay points out, this book gives a reassuring picture of the man of faith happily co-existing with the radical Biblical critic in the one and the same personality.

PERSECUTION IN THE EARLY CHURCH
H. B. Workman

We greet this book with enthusiasm and with gratitude, because it still remains far and away the best and the most thrilling account of the sufferings and the triumphs of the Early Church.[1]

There is a first-class chapter on 'The Causes of Hatred', in which the reasons why the Early Church was persecuted are analysed. (1) The Jews were behind much of the persecution. Tertullian called them 'the sources of persecution'. (2) The superstition of the heathen caused much persecution. The old religion had ceased to be a vital force in Rome, but its observance was still 'a branch of the civil service primarily connected with the safety of the state'. To fail to observe it was to risk the disfavour of the neglected gods. (3) Christians were hated for the effect of Christianity on the family. 'Tampering with family relationships' was one of the earliest charges against the Christians. There were obvious difficulties if one member became a Christian and another did not. (4) The Christian attitude to property, especially to slaves, was bound to cause trouble. In the eyes of Roman law a slave was not a person but a thing. (5) The Christian preaching which looked forward to the end of the world in flames and the destruction of their enemies did not make them popular. (6) The Christian rites were deliberately misunderstood. The Christians were accused of sexual orgies because they kept the Love Feast, the Agapē; the kiss of peace was misunderstood and could indeed be abused; the talk of eating the body and drinking the blood of Jesus Christ produced the charge of cannibalism; the bringing of a child for baptism begot the story that the child was sacrificed. (7) The Christian was necessarily different. There were trades and professions in which he would rather starve than take part. (8) The greatest cause of hatred was that the Christians were regarded as politically disloyal and dangerous because they would not acknowledge the Emperor as Lord, a title which they would give to Christ and to Christ alone.

There is a thrilling chapter on 'The Experiences of the Persecuted'. They were tortured in ways which hardly bear relating, but they remained steadfast. When Carpus was nailed to the Cross he smiled. 'What made you laugh?' said his astonished executioners. 'I saw the glory of the Lord, and was glad', came the answer.

For many years I personally have been urging people to read this book and to see the cost of this blood-bought faith which we hold.

It is to be noted that this paperback edition does not contain the long and scholarly footnotes with which the original edition was equipped. We recognize the impossibility of printing them in an edition like this, but, although the scholar will regret their absence, it will make little difference to the general reader.

This is a good example of how an excellent book never dates. Workman's volume first appeared fifty-four years before this review, which is concerned with an abbreviated re-issue of it. Barclay hails it for the best of reasons: that it makes clear the why's and the wherefore's of the sufferings of the early Church; of the

[1] Published in 1906, it was re-issued in 1959 as a 'Wyvern Book' by EPWORTH PRESS.

reasons for the persecution of Christians in the early centuries of the faith; and the triumphs with which they overcame them. Oddly enough, this is a task rarely attempted and Barclay, as a lifelong student and teacher of the early Christian scene, is obviously gratified at the re-appearance, of a classic.

THE ARK OF GOD
D. Stewart

There have always been two attitudes in the Church to secular literature. On the one hand, Clement of Alexandria is a mine of quotation from secular authors, and many pagan writers survive only in quotation in his works. His quotations are to be numbered by the thousand. On the other hand, Tertullian violently demanded what Jerusalem had to do with Athens, and what the Christian had to do with secular literature. For him secular culture was a forbidden territory.

The Rev. Douglas Stewart has given us a fascinating study of the Christian apologetic which can be found in modern literature and in the most unlikely places.[1] In this book there are studies of five modern novelists—James Joyce, Aldous Huxley, Graham Greene, Rose Macaulay and Joyce Carey. All these he says have been 'practising a new kind of apologetic, an apologetic not of the schools but of the stage, the screen, the novel. In the forefront they have set not dogmas, not documents, but human beings, and the argument has been carried on not in terms of reason, but in terms of life'. Mr. Stewart insists, and rightly, that we are bound in common sense to embark on 'some examination of these lay preachers who succeed in discussing sin and salvation on the West End stage before audiences who turn a deaf ear to these themes when they are introduced by a clerical voice'.

Mr. Stewart quotes with approval the words of W. B. J. Martin about what constitutes a 'religious' book. Such a book is the product of a certain attitude to life. It takes the human predicament seriously; it is the product of a deep compassion. 'It is informed and suffused with a great pity for man in his plight; it sees man, not men; the individual in his solitariness, not types or stock characters. It may not use religious terminology or quote the words of Jesus, but it stands where He stood.

Mr. Stewart sees in James Joyce something of what Tillich meant when he spoke of the three fears of man—the fear of death which was typical of the classical world, the fear of guilt which agonized the Middle Ages, and the fear of meaninglessness which is characteristic of the modern world.

In Huxley there is an essential mysticism. 'Nothing in the mechanics of the ear explains Bach or our ecstasy.' 'Man', in Sir Thomas Browne's famous definition, 'is the great amphibian', inhabiting both the world of time and the world of the spirit.

The most interesting thing about Graham Greene is that, devout Roman Catholic though he is, he can draw pictures of priests and of the Church which are apparently harsher than any Protestant would draw.

We can do no more than indicate what is in this very interesting and important book. It will lead many a reader into realms into which he has not previously penetrated; and the reader will suddenly become aware that Saul is among the prophets and that the Christian faith has allies in places where such allies were little to be expected.

In this book Douglas Stewart, a Baptist, and one-time Assistant Head of Religious Broadcasting in the B.B.C., sets out to explore modern literature for traces, conscious or unconscious, of the

[1] Published by CAREY-KINGSGATE PRESS.

Christian apologetic. It was an original idea. Rightly, Barclay described it as an 'interesting and important book'. He also leaves us in his debt by picking out the penetrating remark that the fear of death was typical of the classical world, the fear of guilt agonized the Middle Ages, and the fear of meaningless is characteristic of the modern world.

OBJECTIONS TO CHRISTIAN BELIEF
A. R. Vidler (Ed.)

It is a long time since Plato said that the unexamined life is the life not worth living; and it is equally true that the unexamined faith is the faith not worth having. Here the Christian faith is subjected to the most stringent examination by a group of fearless Christian thinkers.[1]

The book has four sections: 'Moral Objections', by D. M. Mackinnon; 'Historical Objections', by A. R. Vidler; 'Psychological Objections', by H. A. Williams; 'Intellectual Objections', by J. S. Bezzant. The names of the authors are guarantee of the scholarship within it. The chapter which we propose here to outline is that on 'Historical Objections' by A. R. Vidler.

There are two opposing views of Christianity. First, there is the view that Christianity is tied to history. Professor Mascall writes: 'It has often been emphasized that Christianity is historical in a sense in which no other religion is, for it stands or falls by certain events which are alleged to have taken place during a particular period of forty-eight hours in Palestine nearly two thousand years ago'. Second, there is the view that it is quite impossible to tie Christianity to history. G. L. Dickinson said: 'My difficulty about Christianity is and always has been that Christians make the centre of their faith the historical existence of a man at a certain age. I dare say he *did* exist, though that has been doubted. But if he *did*, what was he really like?

And yet it will make a difference to believe that God did invade actual history at an actual time. But what are the difficulties?

First, no truth of history can be other than highly probable. This is true. But there is a difference between saying, 'It is certain', and 'I am certain'. We continually act on a personal certainty even when an objective certainty is not possible.

Second, if there is universal agreement about a fact, and if we could examine the evidence for ourselves and come to a conclusion, then certainty would be much easier to obtain.

Third, in any event no historian writes without bias, although there is a world of difference between the historian who takes a thesis to the facts and an historian who allows a thesis to emerge from the facts.

But there is another side. First, the results of Christianity are so stupendous that it may well be argued that there is a stupendous event at the heart of them. Second, Christian events must in the last analysis be viewed from within Christian experience.

Dr. Vidler ends with an appeal to the non-believer to examine his beliefs and non-beliefs as stringently as Christian belief is examined in this book, and to the believer to remember that there are many ways and many degrees of certainty to and in Christian belief.

This is an intensely important book. Any thinking Christian who reads it will be better able to face himself, the world, and God.

In their day, some sixteen years or so ago, the lectures upon which this book is based made a considerable stir. One of them, on historical objections to Christian belief, was delivered by A. R. Vidler, at that time Fellow and Dean of Kings College. It is this particular contribution which Barclay has selected for especial notice. As he says, this is

[1] Published by CONSTABLE in 1963.

an importance book because the issue is so important. How historical is Christianity? Since these lectures were delivered in Cambridge we have become more attuned to the free-ranging examination of fundamental issues which they represent. For a comment on the ever burning issue of the historicity of Christianity, we would still do well to read Barclay's comments, and to remember that much of his own writings have been directed to this same end.

THE CHURCHES AND THE LABOUR MOVEMENT
S. Mayor

The proverb has it: 'The more things change, the more they remain the same'. This thought has constantly been in my mind as I read Stephen Mayor's book.[1] There is not a problem which faces the Church today which did not face it just as acutely a hundred years ago.

There is the problem of falling attendance. A census of Church attendance was taken in 1886 and again in 1903. Between the two censuses the population of the country had increased by half a million, and yet the Anglican Church attendance had dropped from 535,715 to 396,196, and the Nonconformist from 369,349 to 363,882.

There is the problem of the drift of the working-classes from the Church. In 1866 the newspaper *The Nonconformist* wrote that the working-classes 'are almost wholly beyond the range of our religious institutions'.

The Church's gospel was that people should stay as they are. The *Nonconformist* in 1873 said that it was part of the creed of bishops 'to teach men to be satisfied with the conditions in which they have been born'.

Certain sections of the Church were against all rises in wages. *The Nonconformist* said that you could no more legislate for hours of work and for wages than you could legislate for the weather. The *Church Family Newspaper* characterized Old Age pensions as 'bribing the democracy to be thriftless'.

The same newspaper protested against meals in schools for hungry children. Start it and the demand will never stop. 'If the children are to be fed, they must be medically inspected; then they must be clothed, and after that will come fresh claims.'

In the Church the poor were segregated in the few free seats available for them, behind pillars and in remote corners. Prominent Christians so-called like Lord Overtoun passionately preached Sabbath Observance and mercilessly worked their employees on Sundays in shocking conditions.

Of course, there was another side in which the Church, especially the Nonconformist Church, was in the van of progress, and many of the great Labour leaders grew up in the Church: William Abraham; Arthur Henderson; George Lansbury, Will Crooks and Keir Hardie, for example.

Even those who were not orthodox in belief were not unbelievers. Beatrice Webb still believed in 'something above and around us which is worthy of absolute devotion and devout worship'. Of John Ruskin it was said by one of his biographers: 'His fundamental beliefs were two: the existence of God and the divine quality of beauty.'

Certainly in the Church's record there was much of shame, but there was much of glory too, and from the Church the Labour Movement drew much of its inspiration and its manpower. We owe Mr. Mayor a real debt of gratitude for this book which is comprehensive, interesting and always meticulously documented. This book shows how fascinating for the general reader the product of careful research can be made.

The time when the Anglican Church was said to be 'the Conservative Party at prayer', or when non-conformity could adopt the attitudes toward the working

[1] Published by THE INDEPENDENT PRESS, 1967.

class which are here attributed to it in Barclay's quotations from the book, is long past. In Spain, in South America, in Africa (with the notable exception of South Africa), and in many areas of Western Europe, the Churches seem to be increasingly in the forefront of critics of the established régimes and systems. It is a long time indeed since, as The Nonconformist claimed in 1873, it was part of the creed of Bishops 'to teach men to be satisfied with the conditions in which they have been born'.

PERSONAL EVANGELISM
Cecil Pawson

It is generally true to say that only a man who has done something has the right to tell others how to do it. If any man has a right to write about personal evangelism that man is Professor H. Cecil Pawson and he has done so.[1] For thirty-six years Professor Pawson has met his men's club every Tuesday evening, and every Saturday evening has been given to personal interview. It is out of experience that he speaks.

Professor Pawson has no doubt what evangelism is. To become a Christian is 'to respond to the love of Christ', and therefore evangelism is to confront men with that love. Professor Pawson sees the danger of losing this definition. Evelyn Underhill once wrote of some people that they 'desert Christ and enter His service instead'. Those who, for instance, run youth clubs must beware lest, 'Our evangelism is lost in our friendship'. Professor Pawson never loses sight of what is to him the primary aim of evangelism.

Professor Pawson is of the opinion that 'it is harder to make a convert now than twenty years ago or even ten years'. He feels that men are nowadays 'less aware of the existence of God, heaven and hell'. 'Two world wars, the decline in church attendance, the passing of family prayers, the neglect of Bible reading, the diminishing attendance at Sunday School, the failure of parental example and discipline have all tended more and more to produce a godless age.' The situation demands action. Paul's advice was, 'Do the work of an evangelist', not call a conference or set up a committee. And it requires action now. 'There is much wisdom in Pepy's remark in his famous diary: "Nobody beginning, I did".'

Professor Pawson is sure, and rightly sure, that all problems are theological problems. He therefore begins by outlining the spheres in which the Gospel is needed—in the world of education, in the world of science, in the world of industry, in the world of politics, in the medical world, in the world of international relations, in the world of the space age, in the world of home life. He is also sure of the individual nature of evangelism. The ultimate aim must be 'persons committed to Christ'.

This book abounds in wise sayings which could be seeds for the preacher and the teacher. To Christ we bring 'the past to be forgiven, the present to be strengthened, the future to be guided'. He sees on the Cross the love 'which will never let us go, never let us off, and never let us down'.

Professor Pawson quotes the saying of Dean Inge: 'There's not much difference between one man and another, but what there is is very important'. Vernon Bartlett writes in his book *Tuscan Retreat*: 'In the final analysis what is any of us doing but killing time until time kills us?' Professor Pawson reminds us—very usefully—of Lord Soper's saying that in any religious argument it is tragically possible to win your argument and to lose your man.

This is a wise, a stimulating, a challenging, and above all a gracious book by a man who knows and loves what he is writing about.

A stimulating and challenging book; as Barclay points out, the writer has certainly earned the right to speak as one who has been involved in personal evangelism with his men's

[1] Published by EPWORTH PRESS, 1968; re-issued as a paperback in 1975 by ST. ANDREW PRESS.

club for thirty-six years. Barclay, as ever, has the eye for the striking quotation, such as this from Dean Inge: 'there's not much difference between one man and another, but what there is is very important'.

THE NEW TESTAMENT AND CRITICISM
George Eldon Ladd

There can be no doubt that it makes a difference who wrote a book, this is specially true of this book. The outstanding fact is that it is written by one of the notable conservative scholars of our time, and it is an honest attempt by one who is and who remains a conservative to come to terms with the uses and the values of modern critical scholarship.

The tension is between what we may call the fundamentalist and the liberal. The fundamentalist takes a 'high' view of the Bible; he insists on the virgin birth, the deity of Christ, the reality of the miracles, the vicarious death of Christ, the bodily resurrection of Christ, the second coming, and the plenary view of Scripture. He takes the Bible 'as it stands'. On the other hand, there are indeed liberals who seem to equate scholarship and destruction, who leave no room for the supra-natural and the supra-historical. The result is that the fundamentalist tends to be suspicious of, and even hostile to, all so-called critical scholarship, while to the liberal he seems to be an obscurantist, and fundamentalist and even conservative scholarship tends to be largely 'devotional, popular, apologetic and defensive'. Professor Ladd wishes to bridge this unhappy divorce—and in my opinion he succeeds magnificently in his task.

Professor Ladd's view of Scripture is 'high'; on this he concedes nothing. But his view of Scripture which he repeats again and again, is all-important: 'The Bible is the Word of God given in the words of men in history'. He quotes the saying of a conservative: 'I am glad that we find in the Bible the Word of God, not the words of men'—a truth, but a half-truth. 'The Bible *is* a compilation of the words of men. Each book of the Bible was composed by some one at a given time in a definite place, even though the author, date and provenance are now unknown.' Revelation is 'God's word spoken to men, and then expressed in the words of men'. 'Evangelicals cannot be satisfied simply to recognize and defend the Bible as the Word of God; they must examine thoroughly the dimensions of the Bible as the words of men.' It is thoroughly legitimate to discuss, say, the authorship of the first gospel or of the Pastorals, or the structure of the Corinthian correspondence. If from no other fact, the human element in the Bible can be seen in the fact that each author writes in his own literary style.

History, linguistics, archaeology, literary criticism must all be laid under tribute; not to destroy but to understand the Bible. 'In the search for a good text (of the Bible) piety and devotion can never take the place of knowledge and scholarly judgment. One does not solve a problem of divergent textual readings by prayer or by the inner illumination of the Holy Spirit, but only by an extensive knowledge and skill in the science of textual criticism.' 'Questions of historical philology are not answered by the depths of a student's religious devotion, nor by his theological convictions. On the contrary, the positions taken by systematic theology must rest on the findings of scientific philology.'

The chapter on Textual Criticism is as masterly a summary of the facts and conclusions as I have ever seen. And it is written in the conviction that, 'Of all people, evangelicals who believe in an inspired scripture should insist on the greatest possible accuracy in the text. It is a strange anomaly that those who have most strongly emphasized the importance of verbal inspiration have often been the very ones who have most highly revered the English Bible which possesses a very inaccurate text'.

When we study the differing reports of the words of Jesus in the gospels, we are presented with a phenomenon which makes a 'dictation' theory of inspiration impossible; and we are to see that it was not the *words* but the *substance* of Jesus' teaching in which the gospel-writers are interested.

But Professor Ladd is insistent on one thing—history in the Bible cannot be treated like ordinary history. It is salvation-history. History is the arena of the activity of God. Therefore we cannot insist, for instance like Bultmann, on an unbroken chain of causality in rationalistic terms. There must be supra-historical events, like, for instance, the resurrection.

This is a magnificent book. It has chapters on Textual Criticism, Linguistic Criticism, Literary Criticism, Form Criticism, Historical Criticism, Comparative Religion Criticism. Each chapter is a masterly survey of the subject with a most judicious judgment on the use and abuse of each of them. It should be in the hands of every student, of every minister, and of every inquiring layman. The conservative and the liberal will profit equally from the reading of it—and in that sense it is unique.

We have here the deeply interesting spectacle of Barclay, the so-called liberal biblical scholar, reviewing a book by a man who, if not exactly a fundamentalist, is very nearly so with regard to his position on the Scriptures. Two features are noticeable in Barclay's treatment of this book: first, that he welcomes one who seeks, as this writer does, to bridge the gap between fundamentalist and liberal, and secondly that he finds it possible, to praise the book very warmly indeed. There must be few liberal Biblical critics who are prepared to say of a conservative that his book should be in the hands of every student, of every minister, and of every enquiring layman. And certainly, the writer makes a crucial point when he states, as Barclay emphasizes, that the Bible cannot be treated like ordinary history. It is salvation history.

[1] Published by HODDER & STOUGHTON, 1970.

142

AN INTRODUCTION TO PASTORAL COUNSELLING
K. Heasman

Few ages have been such ages of tension as the latter half of the twentieth century. It is estimated that in Britain at the present time 5000 men and women succeed in committing suicide every year, and another 30,000 to 40,000 attempt to do so. As far back as 1952 it was reliably estimated that there were 350,000 alcoholics in Britain and today the number is certainly very much higher. The increasing problem of addiction to drugs shows the same situation. There is therefore much need for a book such as this.[1]

The problem is maladjustment to life and to its situations. 'Counselling involves a relationship in which one person endeavours to help another to understand and to solve his difficulties of adjustment to society.' Modern counselling is defined as 'assisting an individual to develop insight and ability to adjust to successive events in his life through the appraisal of his capacities, aptitudes and interests; helping him to understand motivations, emotional reactions and compensatory behaviour; and helping him to attain a degree of personal integration whereby he can most effectively use his potentialities and make the greatest contribution to the society in which he lives'.

One of the most serious statements of this book is that people no longer turn instinctively to the parson or the minister for such help. 'They (parsons) are no longer regarded as people who possess a fund of knowledge and wisdom which is generally available. In fact they are often thought to be out of date and out of touch with the ordinary everyday world and its problems.' If this is true, it is even more serious than declining attendance at church.

Man finds life in relationships, and the trouble is that real communication is becoming ever more difficult. People move much more quickly now. 'The average family in Britain changes house once every seven years.' Deep and lasting friendship become thus far less easy. Increasing specialization produces terms and interests which are not easily shared. 'There is a widening gap between the generations.' The changes in traditional ethical and moral values have 'a traumatic effect'. The modern situation begets loneliness.

There are three general methods of counselling—the directive, in which a person is told what to do; the non-directive, in which a person is guided to find out for himself what to do; the eclectic, in which both methods are combined.

The moving thing about this book is its picture of the counsellor. Here are some of the things said about the counsellor, collected from all over the book. The counsellor must learn to 'be' the other person. He must learn to 'see through some one else's spectacles'. He must regard every person and every problem as unique. He must somehow build a bridge between himself and the other person. He must never be shocked. This does not mean that he will always approve, but the other person must always feel that he is accepted in love, no matter what he has to say and to tell. He must learn to have 'a sensitive awareness' of other people. He must learn that it not so much what a person does that matters, but how he takes it into his life and self. His one aim must be to produce dialogue between himself and the other person. He must learn not to be afraid of silence. He must always respect the other person as a

[1] Published by CONSTABLE, 1969.

143

free person. He must make the other person feel that for the moment that person is for the counsellor the only person in the world. Above all, the counsellor must know himself, his faults, his biases, his prejudices; otherwise he cannot help. For helping involves a kind of unique combination of detachment and involvement from and with the other person.

There is much about method and theory in this book, about Adler, Jung, Freud, Buber, about childhood, manhood, age and their problems, about marriage guidance, about individual and group counselling, about counselling and healing. There can be few better books than this for any one who has to deal with others who are in trouble, for it is written out of the fulness of knowledge and experience, but it is also written with what can only be called the simplicity of love.

Barclay comments here on a book by a writer whose major area of concern has been social studies. She was the author of a much acclaimed work Evangelicals in Action, *and has produced other books since then, all of them well received. Barclay certainly sees the value of this book and acclaims it warmly. On the other hand he clearly finds it disturbing, as well he may, that the parson or minister is no longer one to whom people in need of counsel naturally turn. Recent public opinion surveys have indicated, however, that in the last ten years this position may well have changed.*

SECULAR EVANGELISM
F. Brown

George Bernard Shaw once said that the biggest compliment you can pay an author is to burn his books. There are indeed times when disapproval is a more complimentary verdict that approval. Major Fred Brown of the Salvation Army was in charge of the Army's work in the famous Regent Hall in the West End of London. He wrote a book[1] and as a consequence of writing it he lost his command, and on the fly leaf of this book there is the information that the book is written by Major Brown, not as a representative of the Salvation Army, but in his private capacity. If ever there was a book that came straight from the heart of any man, this is it.

Fred Brown was compelled even in reluctance to seek a new way and a new language. He had already been successful in establishing contact with the widest possible cross-section of the community, 'including young drifters. drug abusers, flower children, angry crusaders without a cause, and a growing number of moral and spiritual casualties of our permissive society'. He found his inspiration and his new way in the work and the outlook of Paul Tillich, John Robinson, Dietrich Bonhoeffer, and Harvey Cox.

Fred Brown can see no future for the kind of theology that the usual conservative evangelical holds and the kind of language in which he seeks to propagate it. People neither understand it nor want it. To preach it is 'as useless as trying to sell binoculars in a school for the blind'. But the Christian duty is to 'tell people where to find bread, and then to let them find it for themselves. If we stuff them with bread baked exclusively in our denominational oven, then, despite our sincerity, they will probably be nauseated and develop an allergy'. The trouble is that when orthodoxy is confronted with something new and adventurous 'we scurry down the funk-holes of orthodoxy in the name of defending the faith. . . It is cowardice, the spirit that mistakes bigotry for conviction, and shouts slogans to hide its paucity of thought'.

Fred Brown believes in young people. The one thing about them is that they care and they care intensely. But they are not interested in praying for people; they are interested in giving them bread. They are not interested in God any more; they are done with 'spiritual crutches'. They do not know what you mean by the living Christ, but they are intensely interested in the historic Jesus. They are not interested in talking about what to believe; what matters to them is how to live. When they can be harnessed to service—not to the Church—they can bring to it an 'awe-inspiring self-forgetfulness, compassion, humility and courage'. There is just no question that they display the Christian virtues in a supreme way without the transcendent. It is Fred Brown's conviction that there is no point in trying to talk to them in the old language and with the old theology, because 'they know God by some other name'.

What is needed above all is real involvement. There is a kind of evangelism which looks on people as 'pew fodder'; it is more interested in converts than in persons; it is more interested in talking about human need than in meeting human beings. Fred Brown talks with scorn about the kind of door-to-door campaign which is supposed to be exercising 'personal' evangelism. 'We call such exercises hand-to-hand combat, or, more ludicrous still,

[1] Published by scm press, 1970.

personal contacting, for the whole approach was guaranteed to confirm and strengthen its impersonal nature. People were faces and not personalities. We did not know them or give them the opportunity to know us.'

Fred Brown can say startling things. He writes 'In my Salvation Army officership, I have come across far more unhappiness caused by prayer and its problems than by drunkenness and adultery. He is thinking about the people who feel that they ought to pray as the saints pray—and cannot—people who feel that prayer should mean far more than it does. Very wisely he goes on to say that the surgeon who is operating, and who is so concentrated on his job that he never even remembers God, is worshipping and praying in the realest sense of the term. The one aim of prayer and worship is 'to make us sensitive to the beyond in our midst', and we will find that beyond by giving ourselves —not our money—to the man in need. who is not necessarily in material poverty at all.

It so happens that I know a little about Fred Brown and Regent Hall, for I have had the honour to preach there. And I know that, even if Fred Brown's superiors in 1970 have registered doubt and disapproval, beyond all doubt William Booth would have called him brother. This book is a magnificent confession of real faith.

Major Fred Brown of the Salvation Army, was expelled by the Army as a result of this book. Barclay is therefore on delicate ground but finds himself in no doubt where he stands. 'I know that,' he says 'even if Fred Brown's superiors in 1970 have registered doubt and disapproval, beyond all doubt William Booth would have called him brother.'

1907   Born at Wick, Caithness

1912–25   Educated at Dalziel High School, Motherwell; matriculated *proxime accessit*

1925–29   Read Classics at the University of Glasgow; graduated MA (first class)

1929–32   Read Theology at Trinity College, Glasgow, graduated BD

1932–33   University of Marburg

1933   Married Katherine Barbara Gillespie

1933–46   Minister: Trinity Church, Renfrew

1935   The Bruce Lecturer

1946–63   Lecturer in New Testament Language and Literature in the University of Glasgow

1950   *Ambassador for Christ: The Life and Teaching of St. Paul* (revised 1974)

1952   *And Jesus said* (republished in 1970)

1953–59   *The Daily Study Bible.* (See DSB below)
DSB: The Acts of the Apostles (revised 1976)
DSB: The Gospel of Luke (revised 1975)

1954   *DSB: The Gospel of Mark* (revised 1975)
DSB: The Letters to the Corinthians (revised 1975)
DSB: The Letter to the Galatians (combined with *The Letter to the Ephesians* in 1958, revised 1976)

1955   The Croall Lecturer
And He had compassion on them (republished in a revised edition 1975)
A New Testament Wordbook (republished in a combined volume with *More New Testament Words* in 1964 under the title *New Testament Words*)
DSB: The Gospel of John, volume I (revised (1975)
DSB: The Gospel of John, volume II (revised 1975)
DSB: The Letter to the Romans (revised 1975)
DSB: The Letter to the Hebrews (revised 1976)

1956   The Kerr Lecturer
DSB: The Gospel of Matthew, volume I (revised 1975)
DSB: The Letter to the Ephesians (combined with *The Letter to the Galatians* in 1958, revised 1976)
DSB: The Letters to Timothy, Titus and Philemon (revised 1975)

1957   *Letters to the Seven Churches: A study of the second and third chapters of the Book of Revelation* (revised edition 1969)
DSB: The Gospel of Matthew, volume II (revised 1975)

1958   *The Mind of St. Paul* (republished in 1965)
More New Testament Words (republished in a combined volume, with *A New Testament Wordbook* in 1964, under the title *New Testament Words*)
DSB: The Letters to the Galatians and Ephesians (revised 1976)
DSB: The Letters of James and Peter (revised 1976)
DSB: The Letters of John and Jude (revised 1976)

1959   *Educational Ideas in the Ancient World*
The Plain Man's Book of Prayers
The Master's Men
DSB: The Letters to the Philippians, Colossians and Thessalonians (revised 1975)

147

DSB: The Revelation of John, volume I (revised 1976)
DSB: The Revelation of John, volume II (revised 1976)

1960   *The Mind of Jesus*
           The Promise of the Spirit

1961–69   Co-editor, with Professor F. F. Bruce, of *Bible Guides*

1961   *Bible Guide No. 1: The Making of the Bible*
           Crucified and Crowned

1962   *Flesh and Spirit: A Study of Galatians (5:19–23)*
           Jesus as they saw Him
           More Prayers for the Plain Man
           Prayers for Young People
           The Christian Way

1963–74   Professor of Divinity and Biblical Criticism at the University of Glasgow

1963   The A. S. Peake Memorial Lecturer
           Turning to God: A Study of Conversion in the Book of Acts and Today
           The Plain Man Looks at the Beatitudes
           Many Witnesses, one Lord
           Epilogues and Prayers
           Christian Discipline in Society Today

1964   *The All-Sufficient Christ: A study of Colossians*
           The Plain Man looks at the Lord's Prayer
           Prayers for the Christian Year
           New Testament Words (combining *A New Testament Wordbook* and *More New Testament Words*)

1965   *A New People's life of Jesus*
           Bible Guide No. 20. The Epistle to the Hebrews
           The New Testament in Historical and Contemporary Perspective (co-edited with H. Anderson)

1966   *Fishers of Men*
           The First Three Gospels
           Seen in the Passing

1967   *The Plain Man Looks at the Apostles' Creed*
           Thou shalt not kill

1968   *Prayers for Help and Healing*
           Bible and History: Scriptures in their Secular Setting
           The New Testament: A New Translation. Volume 1 Gospels and Acts
           Communicating the Gospel

1969–70   The James Reid Memorial Lecturer
           The Baird Lecturer
           Sir David Owens Evans Lecturer

1969   *The Lord's Supper*
           The New Testament: a new translation: Volume II The Letters and Revelation
           The King and the Kingdom

1970   Member of the Joint Committee of *The New English Bible* Translation Panel
           Honorary President of the YMCA Glasgow
           Honorary Vice-President of The Boy's Brigade
           God's Young Church

1971   *Through the Year with William Barclay* (edited by Denis Duncan. Parts of which were published in *Marching Orders*, 1973).

1972	*Ethics in a Permissive Society*
	Introducing the Bible
	The Old Law and The New Law
1973	*By What Authority?*
	De Potestate Papae
	Marching Orders (parts of which were previously published in *Through the Year with William Barclay*, 1971)
	The Plain Man's Guide to Ethics
	Everyday with William Barclay (edited by Denis Duncan. Parts of which were published in 1974 under the title *Marching On*)
1974–76	The revised edition of *The Daily Study Bible*
1974	*Jesus Christ for Today*
	Marching On (edited by Denis Duncan. Parts of which were published in 1973 under the title *Everyday with William Barclay*)
1975–76	Visiting Professor of Biology (*sic.*) at the University of Strathclyde
1975	*Testament of Faith* (Autobiographical reminiscences)
1976	*The Men, the Meaning, the Message of the books*
	Biblical Studies: Essays in honour of William Barclay (eds. Johnston R. McKay and James F. Miller)
1977	*Jesus of Nazareth*
	More prayers for Young People